Starfish K2
Learning Linker

Catalogue Publication Data

Starfish K2 Learning Linker
Author: Paul Drury
Pearson Educación de México, S.A. de C.V., 2019
ISBN: 978-607-32-4681-1
Area: ELT
Format: 30.5 x 23.5 cm   Page count: 184

Managing Director: Sergio Fonseca ■ **Innovation & Learning Delivery Director:** Alan David Palau ■ **Regional Content Manager - English:** Andrew Starling ■ **Innovation and Implementation Manager:** Gonzalo Pastor ■ **Publisher:** Hened Manzur ■ **Content Development:** Miroslava Guerra ■ **Content Support:** Susana Moreno ■ **Art and Design Coordinator:** Juan Manuel Santamaría ■ **Design Process Supervisor:** Salvador Pereira ■ **Layout:** Berenice Hinojosa ■ **Cover Design:** BrandB/Fenómeno ■ **Interior Design:** BrandB/Fenómeno ■ **Photo Research:** Salvador Pereira ■ **Photo Credits:** Shutterstock ■ **Illustrations:** Ana Elena García, Belén García Monroy, Carmen López, Gerardo Sánchez, Miguel Angel Chávez, Jaqueline Velázquez, José de Santiago Torices, Olivia González, Thania Dinorah Recio, Ximena García Trigos

The Publisher wishes to acknowledge the valuable collaboration of **Sophie Angerman**, author of the Mathematics program.

© Pearson Educación de México, S.A. de C.V., 2019

First published, 2019

ISBN PRINT BOOK: 978-607-32-4681-1

D.R. © 2019 por Pearson Educación de México, S.A. de C.V.
Avenida Antonio Dovalí Jaime #70
Torre B, Piso 6, Colonia Zedec Ed. Plaza Santa Fe
Delegación Álvaro Obregón, México, Ciudad de México, C. P. 01210

www.pearsonelt.com

Impreso en México. *Printed in Mexico.*

1 2 3 4 5 6 7 8 9 0 - 22 21 20 19

All rights reserved. No part of this publication may be reproduced, stored in a retrieval system, or transmitted in any form or by any means, electronic, mechanical, photocopying, recording, or otherwise, without the prior permission of the publisher.

Pearson Hispanoamérica
Argentina ■ Belice ■ Bolivia ■ Chile ■ Colombia ■ Costa Rica ■ Cuba ■ República Dominicana ■ Ecuador ■ El Salvador ■ Guatemala ■ Honduras ■ México ■ Nicaragua ■ Panamá ■ Paraguay ■ Perú ■ Uruguay ■ Venezuela

Contents

Unit		Page
1	What do you like about yourself?	4
2	Why do we go to school?	24
3	How can you help your family at home?	44
4	Why do you feel hot or cold?	64
5	What other living things are around us?	94
6	Why is food important?	114
7	How can farm animals help us?	144
8	Who lives and works in my town?	164

Read and trace. Draw the picture.

Phonemic Awareness

Learning to Know

an ant

- **Color. Match big and small.**

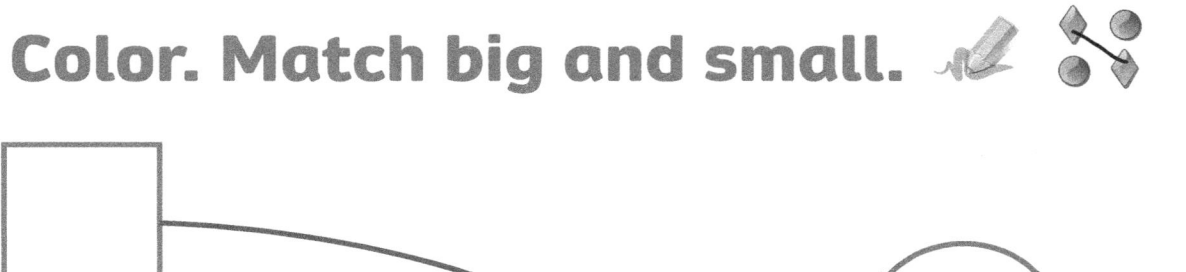

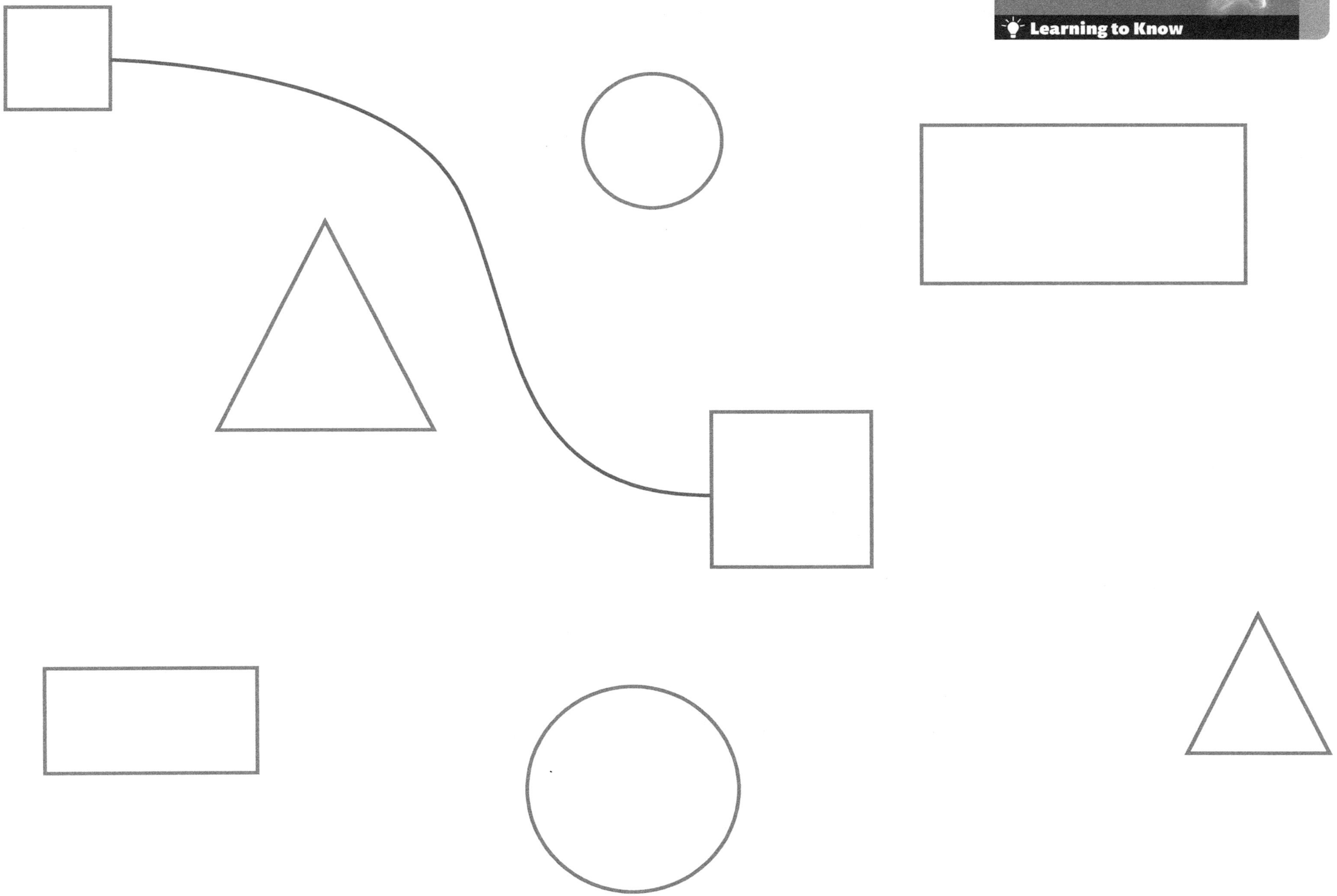

Mathematical Thinking

Learning to Know

Objectives: Name basic shapes. Match big and small shapes in different positions.

Unit 1

- **Which part of the body starts with *a*? Find the word and color.**

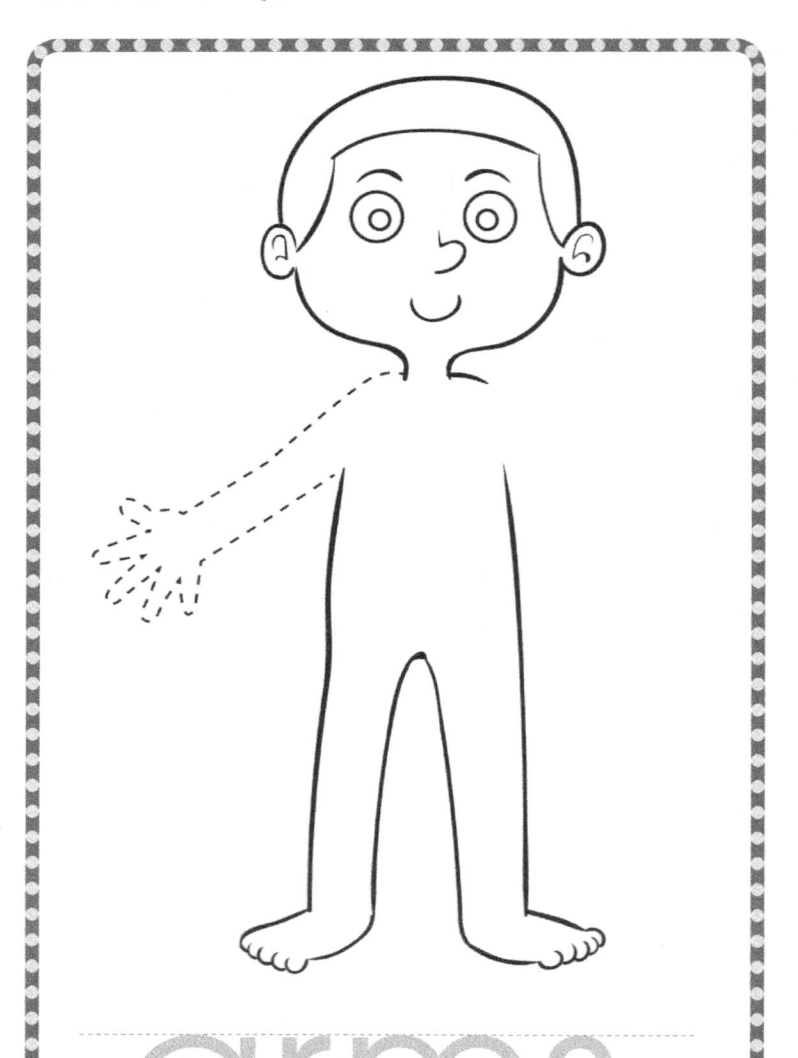

Developmental Writing

Learning to Know

head

arm

arms

- **Draw the arms and trace the word.**

Unit 1

Objectives: Trace *a*.

- **Read and match.**

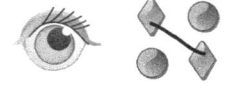

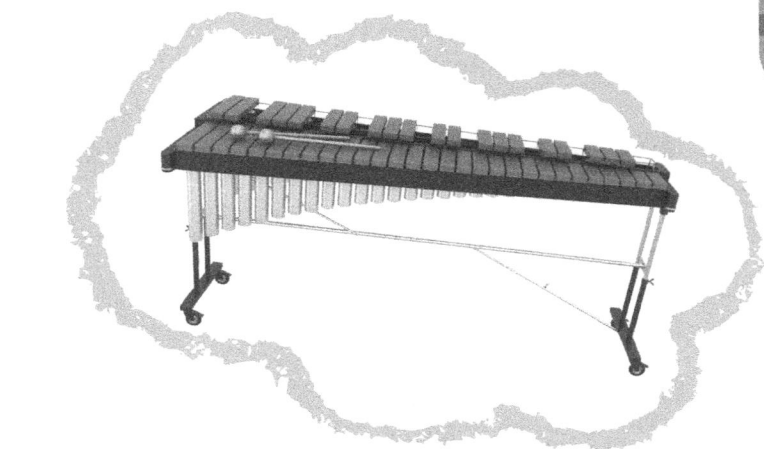

Loud noise

Soft noise

Artistic Expression and Appreciation

Learning to Be

- **Which noise do you like?**

Find more instruments that make a loud noise and instruments that make a soft noise. Draw your favorite instrument.

Objectives: Identify and classify percussion instruments.

Unit 1

7

- **Circle what you need to keep your hair nice.**

Physical Development and Health
Learning to Be

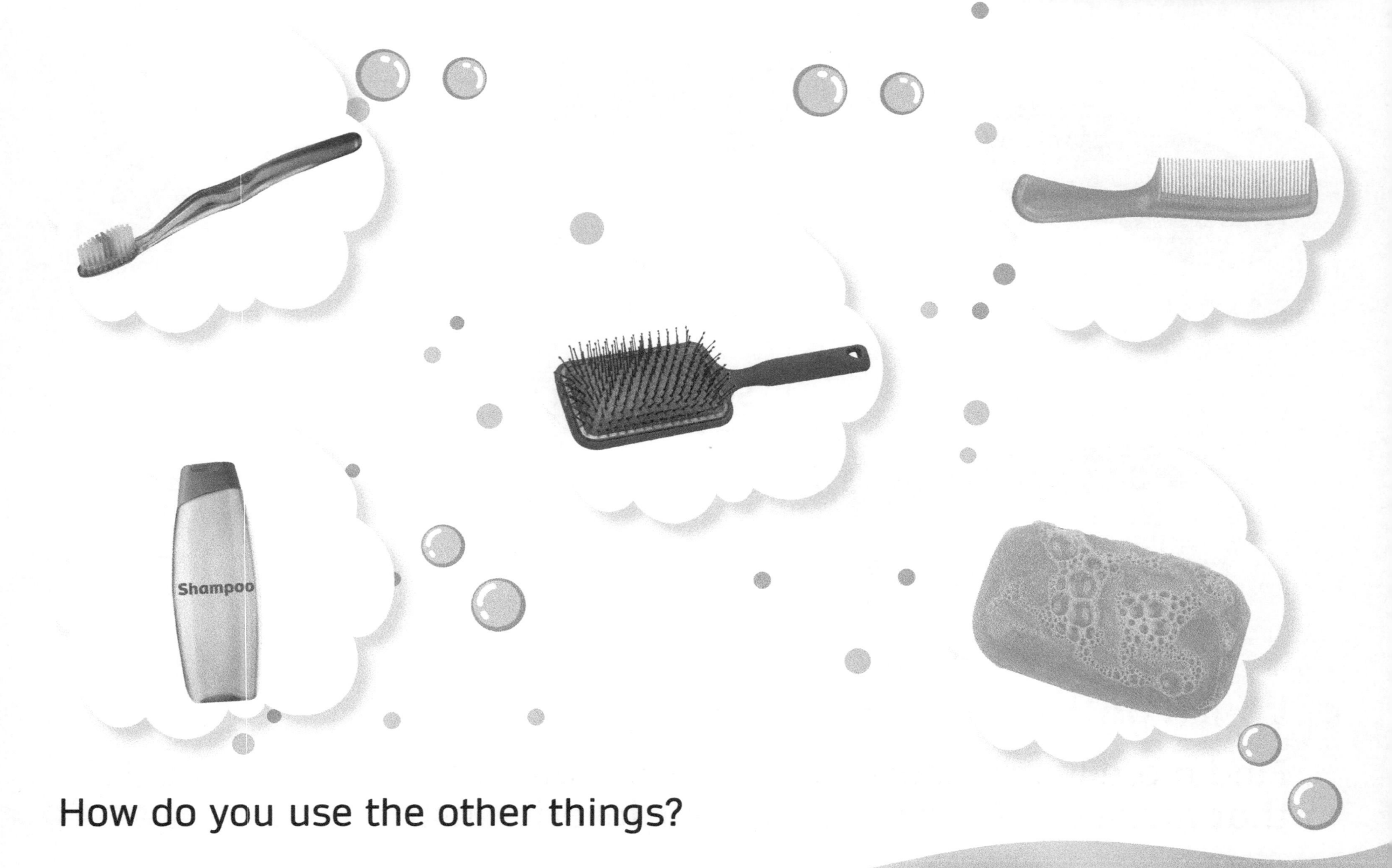

How do you use the other things?

Unit 1

Objectives: Identify things used to look after one's hair.

- **Color the letter e.**

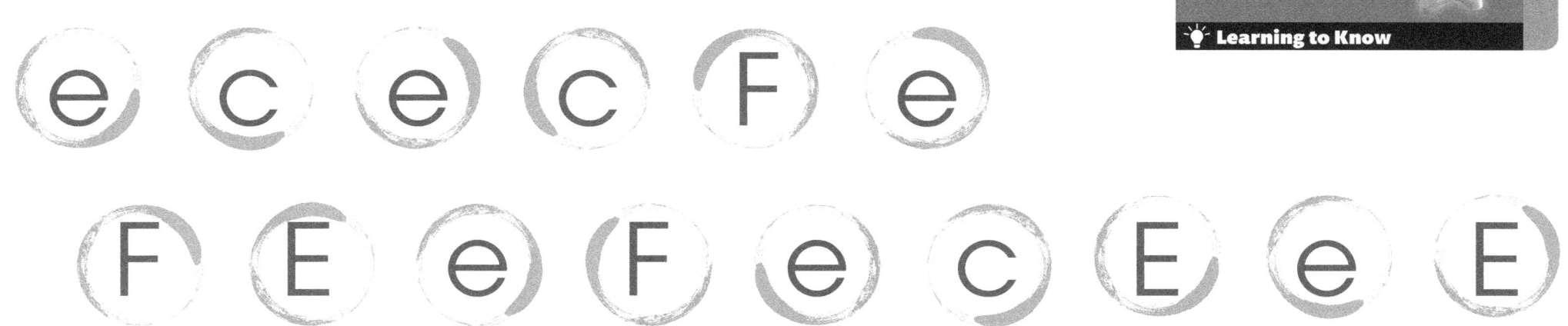

e c e c F e
F E e F e c E e E

- **Now make some e-elephants.**

Unit 1

Objectives: Identify the initial short /e/ vowel sound.

● **Color and trace. Write.**

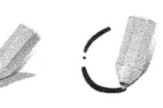

Mathematical Thinking
Learning to Know

1 o 1 1 1 1 1 1 1 1 1
2 oo 2 2 2 2 2 2 2 2 2
3 ooo 3 3 3 3 3 3 3 3 3
4 oooo 4 4 4 4 4 4 4 4 4
5 ooooo 5 5 5 5 5 5 5 5 5
6 oooooo 6 6 6 6 6 6 6 6 6
7 ooooooo 7 7 7 7 7 7 7 7 7
8 oooooooo 8 8 8 8 8 8 8 8 8
9 ooooooooo 9 9 9 9 9 9 9 9 9
10 oooooooooo 10 10 10 10 10 10 10 10 10

10 Unit 1

Objectives: Use a ten-frame. Trace numbers to 10.

- **Match and trace.**

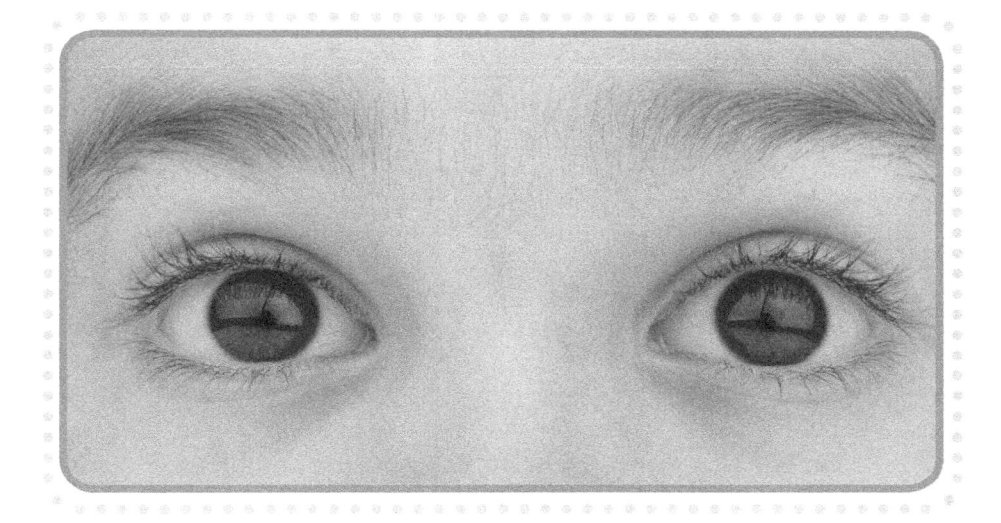

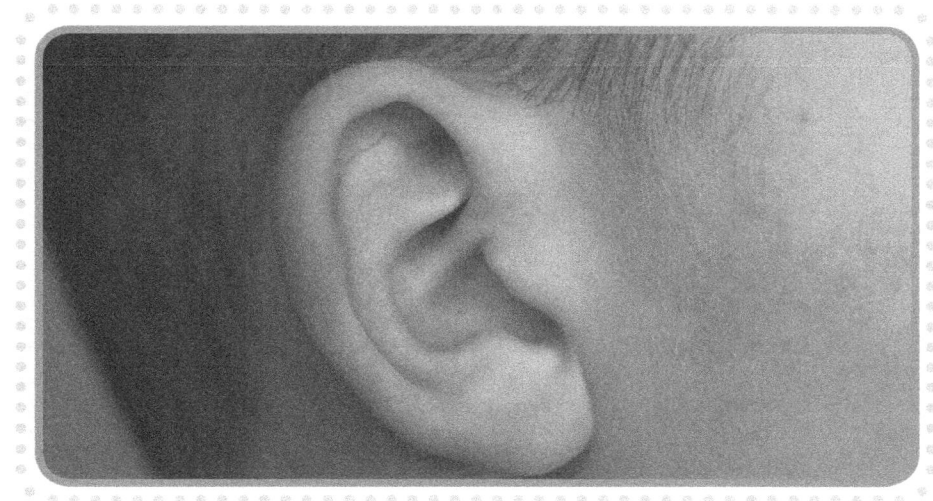

ears

eyes

- **Complete.**

I see with my eyes.

I hear with my ears.

Developmental Writing
💡 Learning to Know

- **Fingerpaint the drawing. Then sing and dance.**

Artistic Expression and Appreciation
Learning to Be

12 Unit 1

Objectives: Express with colors.

- **What's good for your eyes? Check or cross out.** ✔ ✘

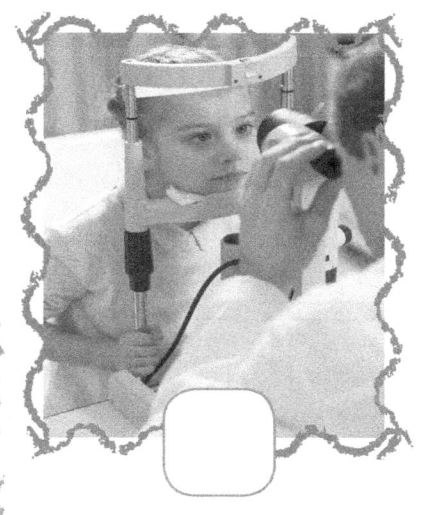

Physical Development and Health
Learning to Be

- **Draw what you do to protect your eyes.**

Unit 1

Objectives: Reflect on how to take care of one's eyes.

- **Decorate the igloo with the letter *i*.**

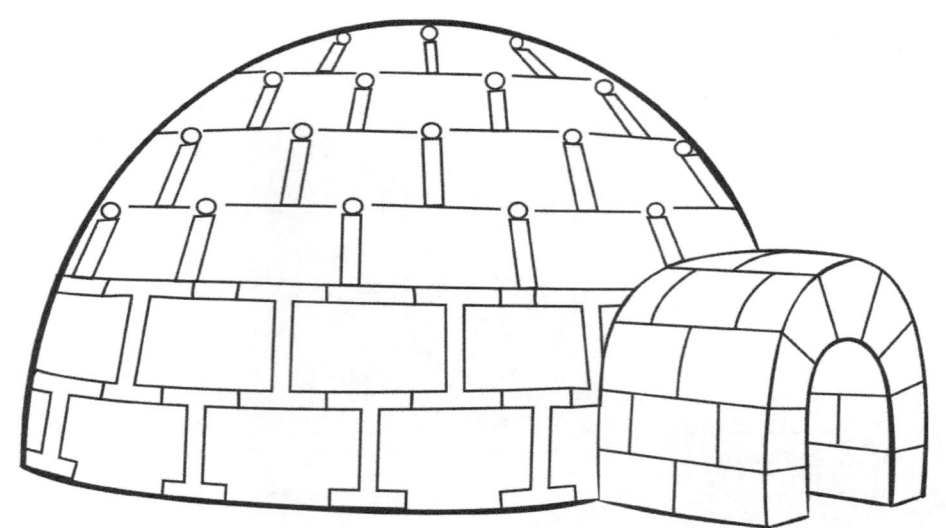

Phonemic Awareness
Learning to Know

- **Circle the letter *i*. Color the iguana blue. Trace.**

An iguana in the igloo.

Objectives: Identify the initial short /i/ vowel sound.

- **Look and say. Complete the pattern.**

- **Draw your own pattern.**

Objectives: Extend and create a simple pattern.

Unit 1

15

- **Trace big *I* and little *i*.**

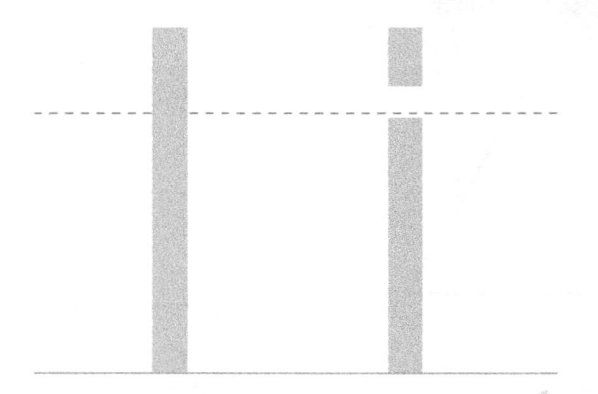

  I i

- **Trace the sentence and read.**

  Put the milk in the fridge.

Unit 1

Objectives: Trace *i*.

- **Color all the letters _I_. What do you see?**

Artistic Expression and Appreciation

Learning to Be

Objectives: Recognize the letter _Ii_.

Unit 1

- **Circle the children that are looking after themselves.**

- **Point and say what you do in the morning.**

18 Unit 1

Objectives: Identify how one can take care of oneself.

Physical Development and Health

Learning to Be

- **Color the *o* in the orange and the *u* in the umbrella.**

Phonemic Awareness
Learning to Know

Objectives: Identify /o/ and /u/ short vowel sounds.

Unit 1

Count. Color. Write.

0 1 2 3 4 5 6 7 8 9 10

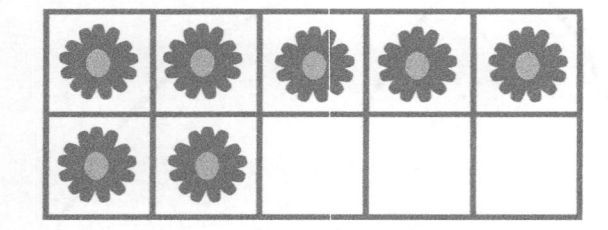

Mathematical Thinking — Learning to Know

7

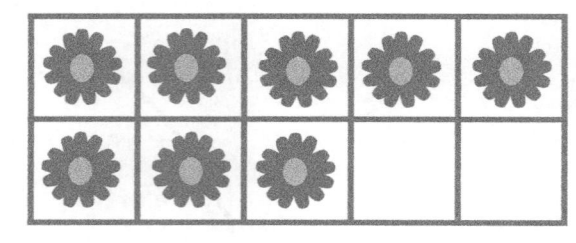

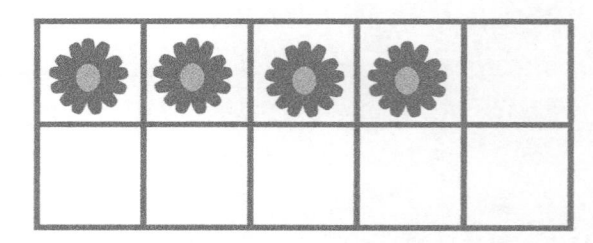

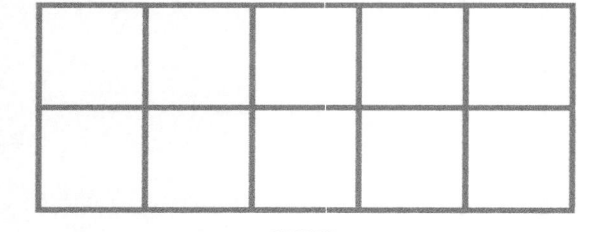

6

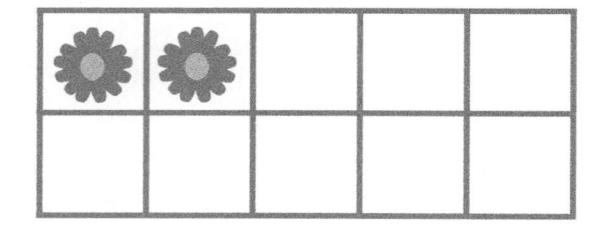

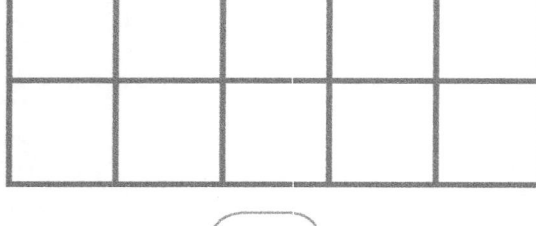

10

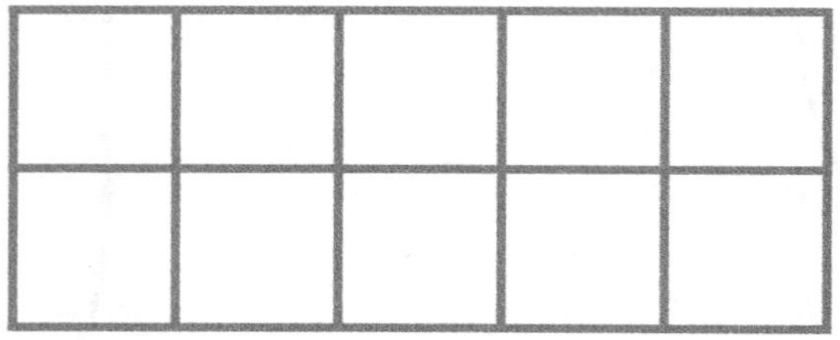

5

- **Match the words to the pictures.**

orange

octopus

ostrich

umbrella

up

unicorn

- **Trace.**

Developmental Writing

Learning to Know

Objectives: Recognize o and u.

Unit 1   21

● **Look and say.**

● **Color the ostrich and the umbrella.**

22 Unit 1

Objectives: Recognize /o/ and /u/ vowel sounds.

Artistic Expression and Appreciation

Learning to Be

Look and number in order.

Physical Development and Health

Learning to Be

Objectives: Learn how to look after one's teeth.

Unit 1

- **Point and say.**

Phonemic Awareness
Learning to Know

Aa

snail

- **Color the objects with the long *a*.**

- **Point, say, trace, and write.**

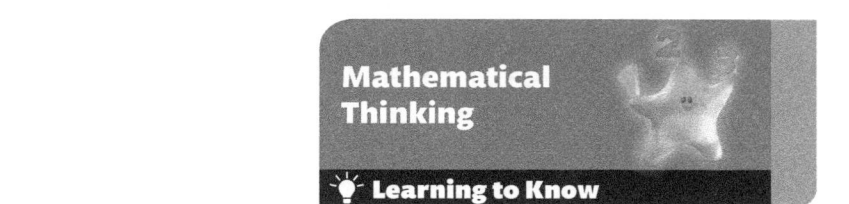

Mathematical Thinking
Learning to Know

1	2	3	4	5	6
7	8	9	10	11	12
	14	15		17	
19		21		23	24
25	26		28		30

Objectives: Rote count to 30. Write missing numbers.

Unit 2

- **Point and say. Then match.**

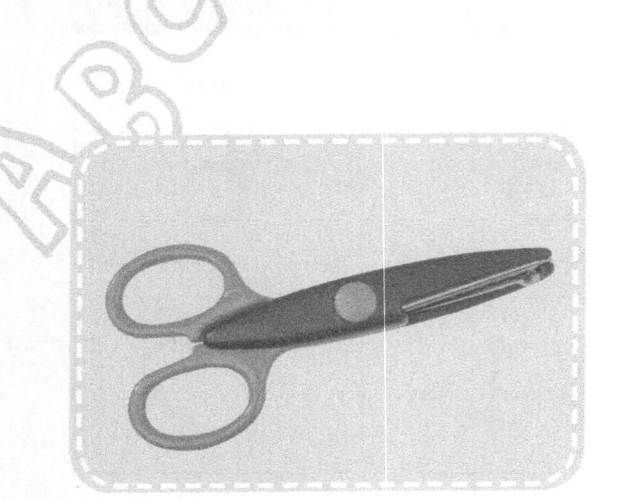

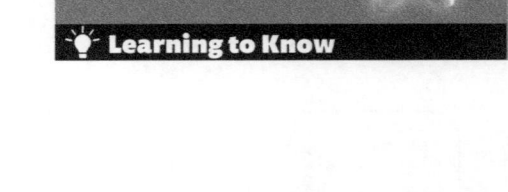

Developmental Writing

Learning to Know

paper

pencil

scissors

table

- **Write the words. Write the long *a* sound using a diferent color.**

26 Unit 2

Objective: Trace words.

- **Look and check the activity you like.**

Artistic Expression and Appreciation
Learning to Be

- **Draw the activity you like the most.**

Objectives: Express likes.

Unit 2

27

- **Circle the children who are looking after their things.**

- **Help clean your classroom.**

- **Point and say.**

Phonemic Awareness — Learning to Know

Ee

leaf

- **Circle the objects with the long e.**

Objectives: Identify the long /e/ vowel sound.

Unit 2

- **Say and trace.**

0 0 0 0 0 0 0   1 1 1 1 1 1 1
2 2 2 2 2 2 2   3 3 3 3 3 3 3
4 4 4 4 4 4 4   5 5 5 5 5 5 5
6 6 6 6 6 6 6   7 7 7 7 7 7 7
8 8 8 8 8 8 8   9 9 9 9 9 9 9
                10 10 10 10 10

- **Trace and count.**

1 2 3 _ _ 6 7 _ _ _

Mathematical Thinking

Learning to Know

Objectives: Write and count up to 10.

- **Match the children to the place.**

- **Complete the words.**

We play.   We eat.

We read.   We color.

Unit 2

Objectives: Identify places at school. Complete words.

- **Are you a boy or a girl? Circle the picture.**

Artistic Expression and Appreciation
Learning to Be

- **Paste paper balls inside the frame.**

Objectives: Make paper balls. Foster fine motor skills.

- **Look and circle what you like to do. Say why.**

- **What do you like? What don't you like? Draw.**

Objectives: Express likes and dislikes.

Unit 2

- **Listen, count, and say.**

  I i

- **Now write the missing long *i*.**

  My kite has n[i]ne p[i]es.

  1, 2, 3, 4, 5, 6, 7, 8, 9. Nine p[i]es.

  Your p[i]e has n[i]ne k[i]tes.

  1, 2, 3, 4, 5, 6, 7, 8, 9. N[i]ne k[i]tes.

Unit 2

Objectives: Identify the long /i/ vowel sound.

- **Point, say, and sort. Draw a line from the object to the word.**

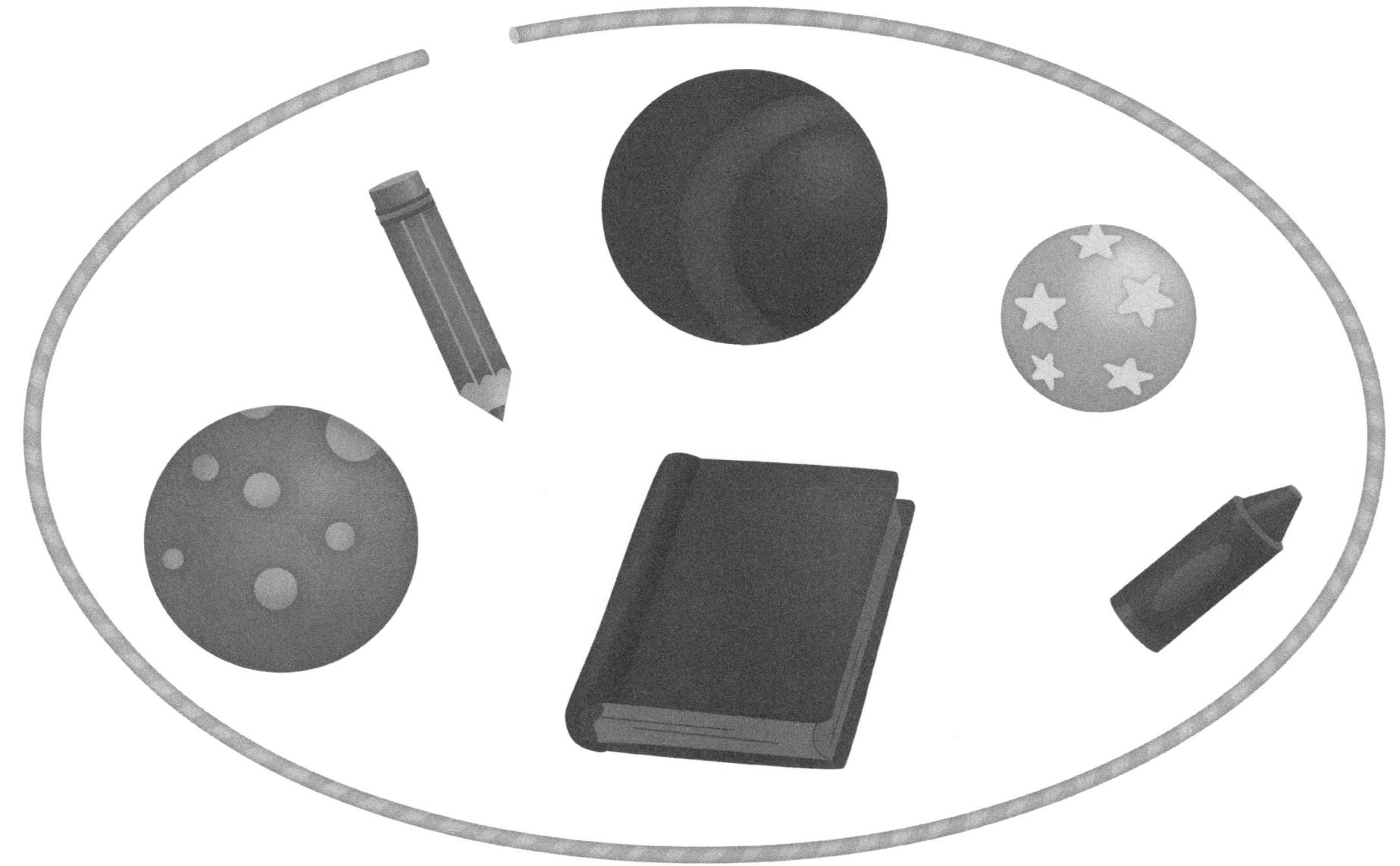

Mathematical Thinking
Learning to Know

round   not round

Unit 2   35

Objectives: Begin to sort objects using one characteristic.

- **Point and say. Then match.**

Open your book.

Sit down.

Close your book.

Stand up.

- **Now write the words.**

Unit 2

Objectives: Trace words related to instructions.

- **Look and say what the children are doing.**

  Artistic Expression and Appreciation
  Learning to Be

- **Draw the objects they are using.**

Objectives: Identify objects.

Unit 2

- **Match the objects.**

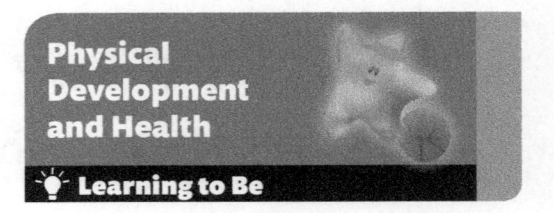

- **Put your supplies away to tidy up the classroom.**

Unit 2

Objectives: Learn to be responsible for school supplies.

- **Circle the words with the long *o* in green.**
  Circle the words with the long *u* in blue.

Phonemic Awareness

Learning to Know

O o

U u

Objectives: Identify long /o/ and /u/ vowel sounds.

Unit 2

Count. Color. Write.

Mathematical Thinking
Learning to Know

0 1 2 3 4 5 6 7 8 9 10 11 12 13 14 15 16 17 18 19 20

17

_____   _____   _____

40   Unit 2

Objectives: Count up to 20.

- **Put the school supplies in the backpack.**

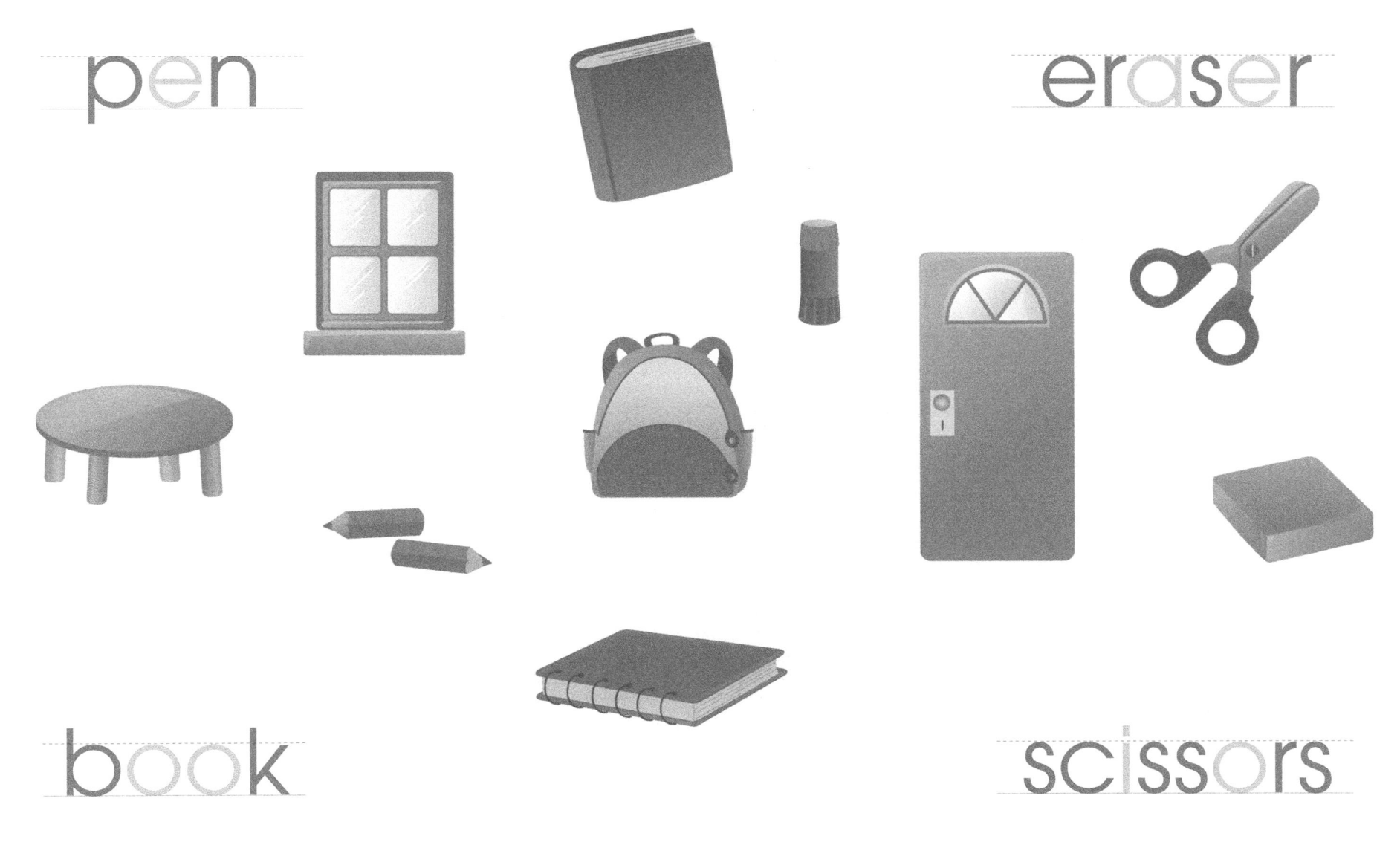

  Developmental Writing
  Learning to Know

  pen

  eraser

  book

  scissors

- **Write the words.**

Objectives: Trace letters to complete words.

Unit 2

- **Look and check the activities you like.**

Artistic Expression and Appreciation
Learning to Be

- **Color in red your favorite activities. Color in green the activities you don't like.**

Objectives: Use colors to express likes and dislikes.

- What do you like more? Color.

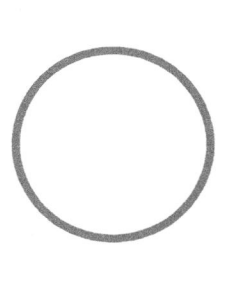

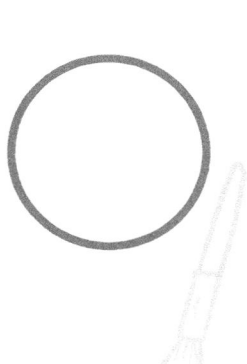

- What do you like? What don't you like? Draw.

Objectives: Express likes and dislikes.

Unit 2

43

- **Trace. Match the letter to the pictures that start with *m*.**

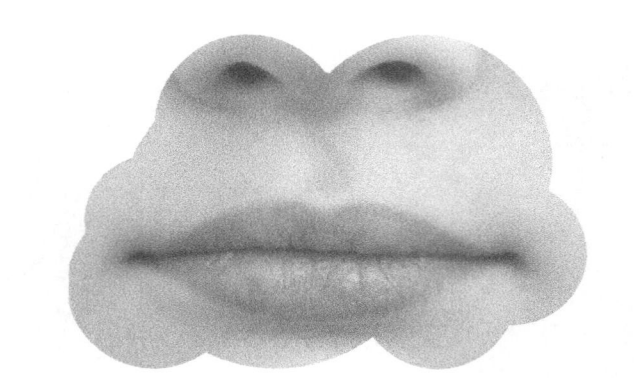

Phonemic Awareness

Learning to Know

Mm

44 Unit 3

Objectives: Identify the initial /m/ sound.

- **Point, say, trace, and write.**

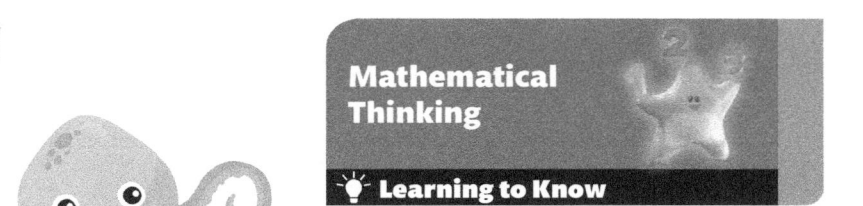

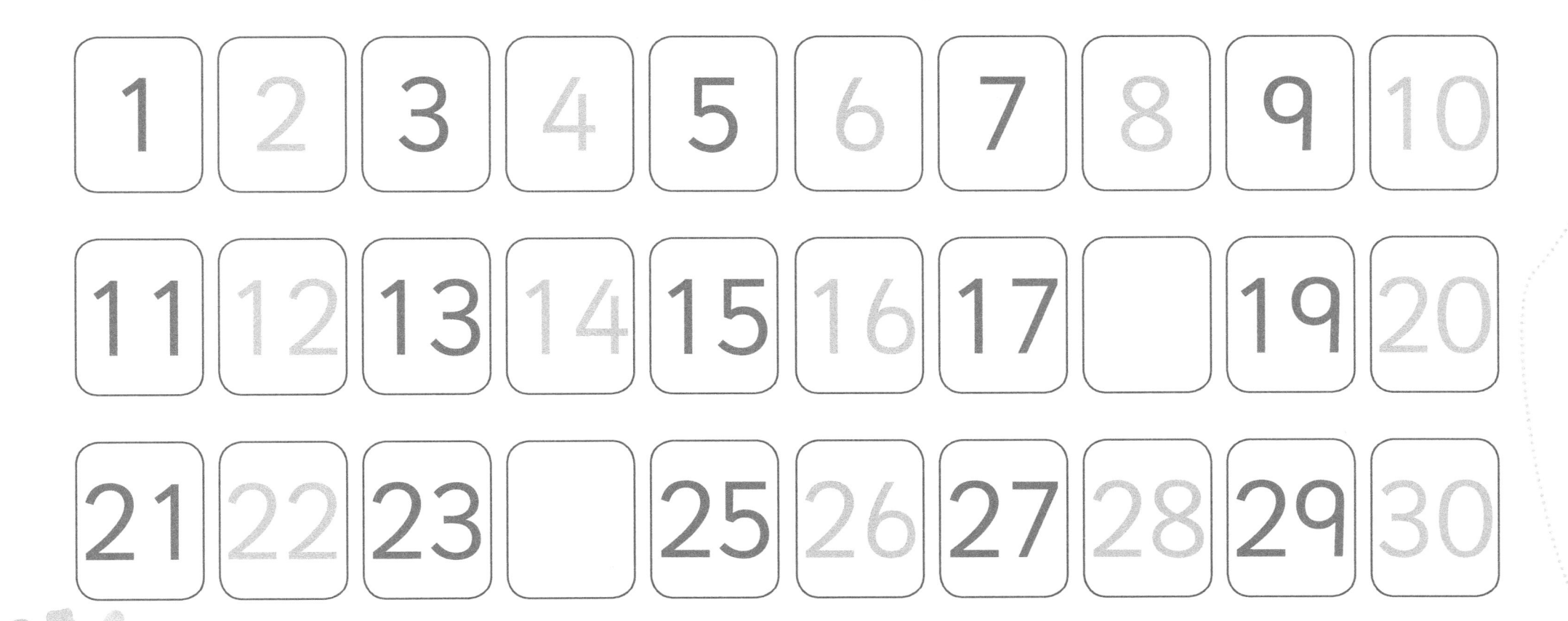

Mathematical Thinking

Learning to Know

1	2	3	4	5	6	7	8	9	10
11	12	13	14	15	16	17		19	20
21	22	23		25	26	27	28	29	30

- **Listen and say. Then write.**

There's a mouse on the mop!

- **Color the correct picture.**

46 Unit 3

Objectives: Identify different words with initial /m/ sound.

- **Match the instrument to the person who is playing it.**

Artistic Expression and Appreciation
Learning to Be

Objectives: Create and play songs.

Unit 3

- **Check the picture that shows the correct action.** ✓

Physical Development and Health
Learning to Be

Objectives: Realize the importance of working together.

- **Circle the words with the s sound.**

Ss

- **Draw another word with the s sound.**

Unit 3

49

Objectives: Identify initial /s/ sound.

• **Look and extend the patterns.**

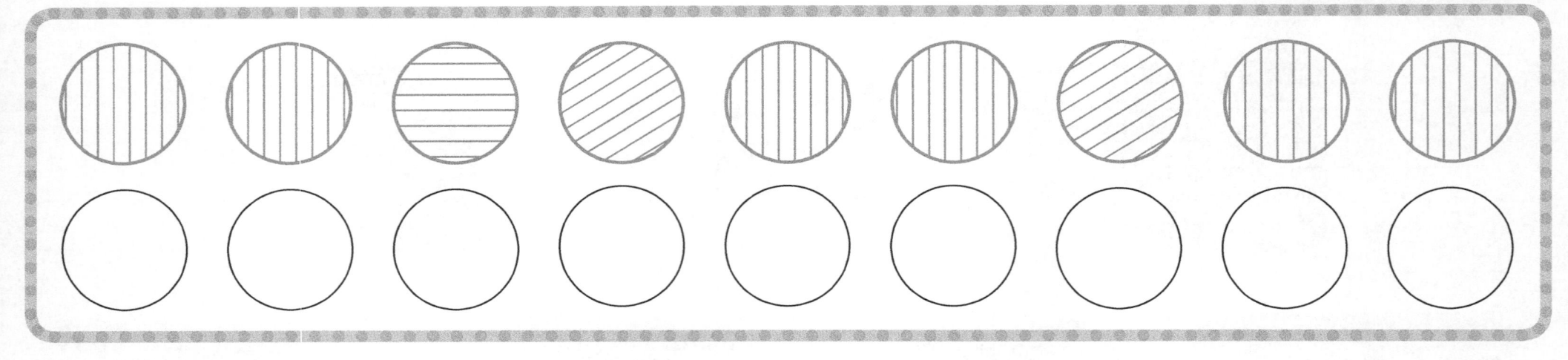

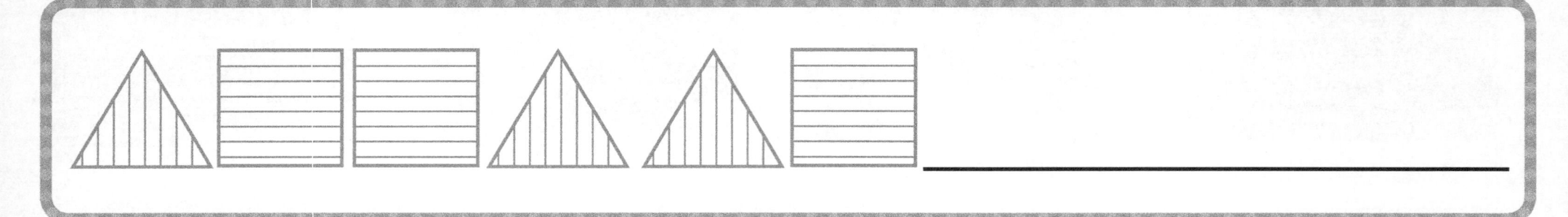

Mathematical Thinking

Learning to Know

50 Unit 3

Objectives: Extend more complex patterns.

- **Match the words to the objects. Trace the letter s.**

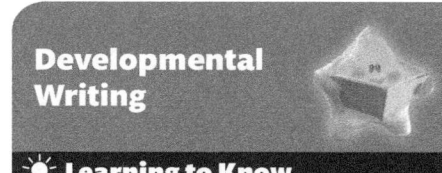

stove

sofa

Sweep, sweep, sweep

- **Color the picture.**

Objectives: Identify words. Trace letter S s.

- **Look at picture 1 and find out what is wrong.**

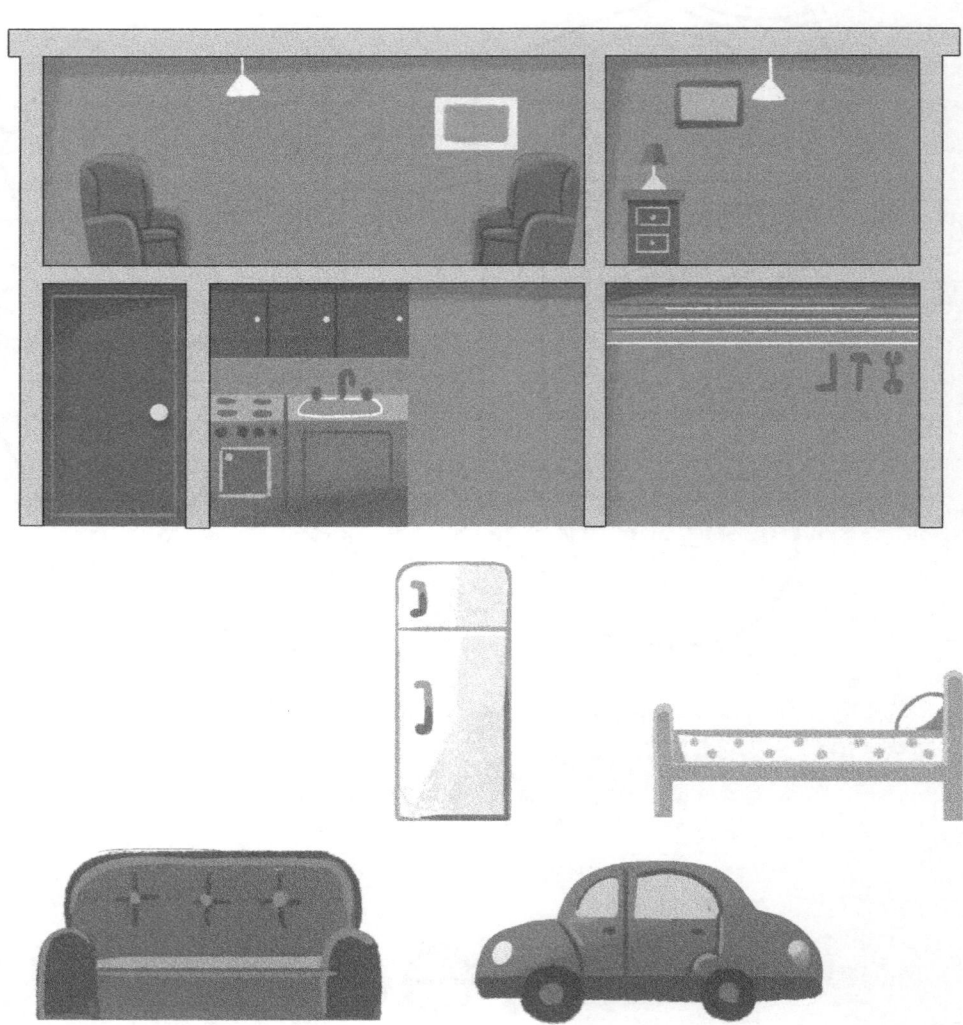

- **Match the furniture to the corresponding room.**

Unit 3

Objectives: Identify the rooms in the house.

- **Look and number the pictures in order.**

Physical Development and Health
Learning to Be

Objectives: Take on different roles and assume responsibility for individual and group tasks.

Unit 3   53

- **Match the words under the pictures to the correct letter.**

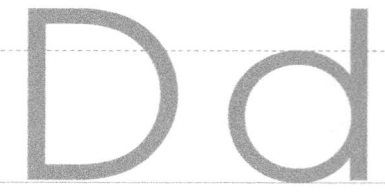

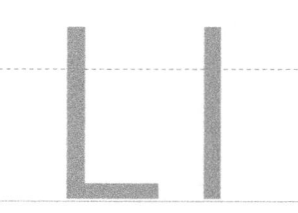

Phonemic Awareness
Learning to Know

light

desk

lemon

Dd   Ll

drum

lion

Dad

54   Unit 3

Objectives: Identify initial /d/ and /l/ sounds.

- **Count and color a square for each item in your home.**

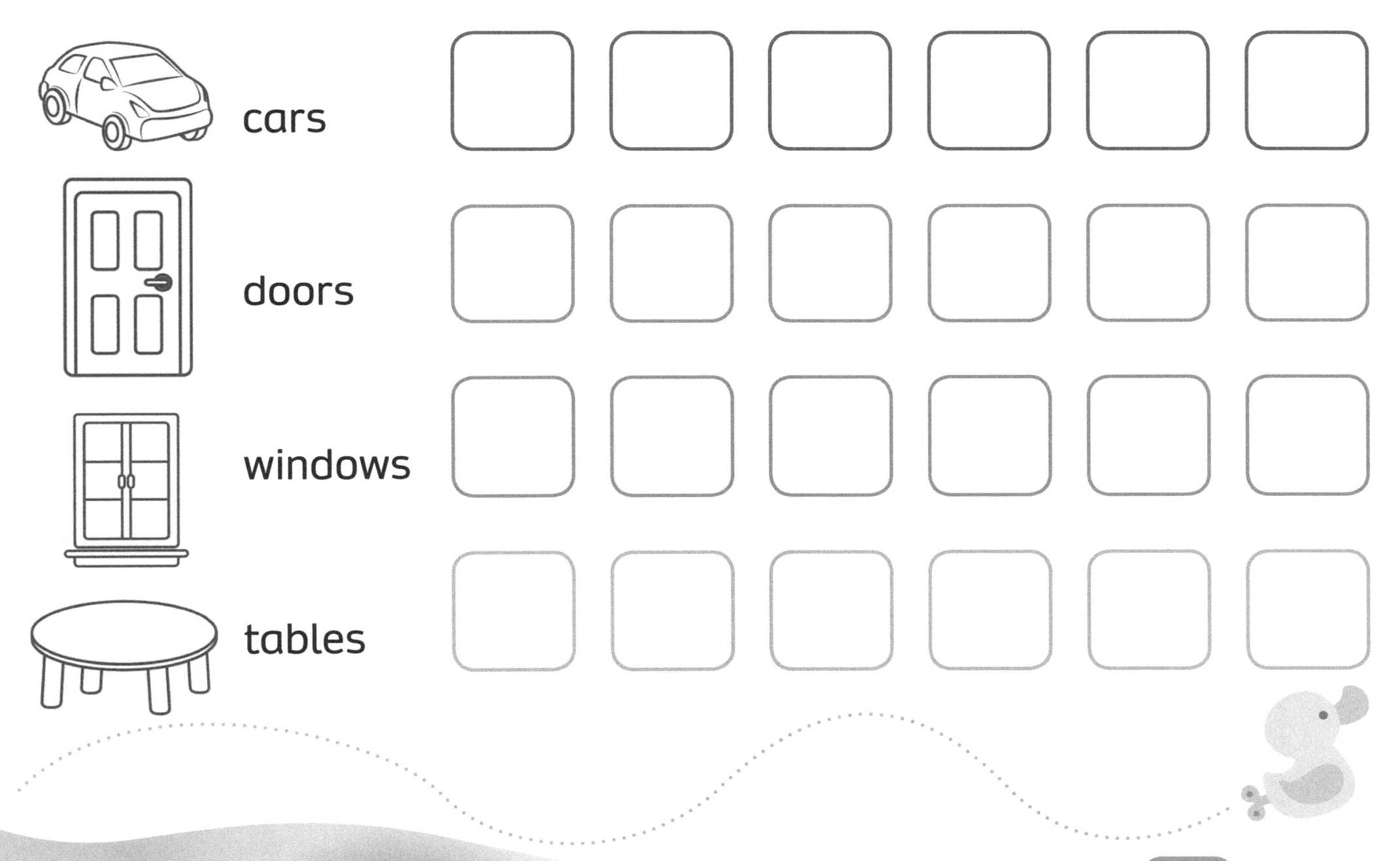

Mathematical Thinking
Learning to Know

cars

doors

windows

tables

Objectives: Can make a simple pictograph.

Unit 3

- **Trace the sentences. Circle the lemon.**

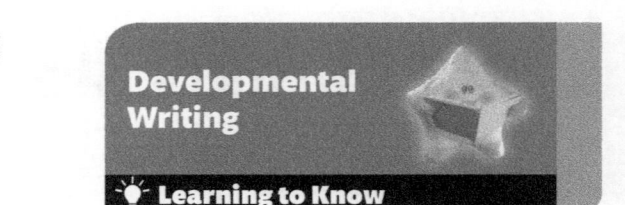

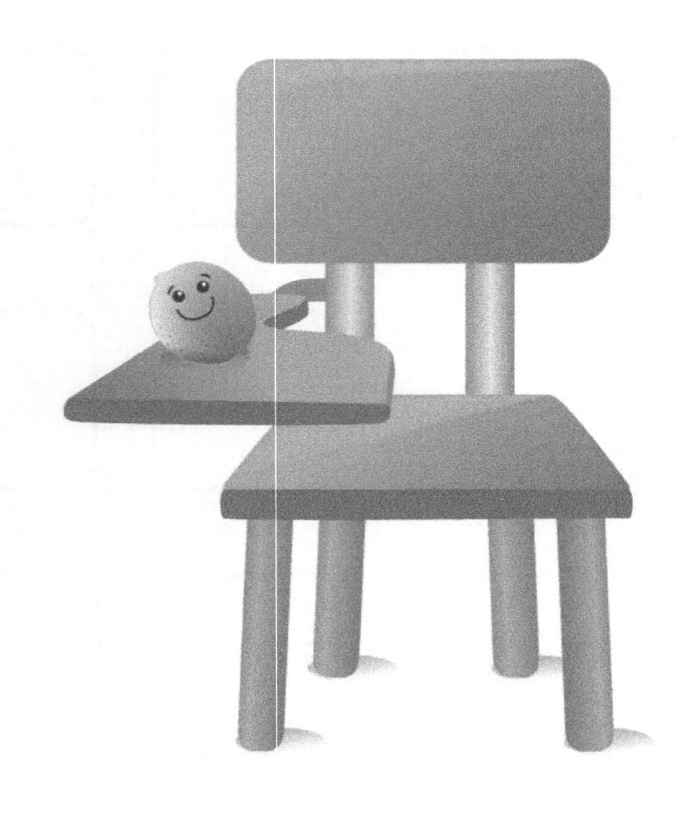

The lemon is on the desk.

The desk is on the lemon.

- **Fingerpaint your family.**

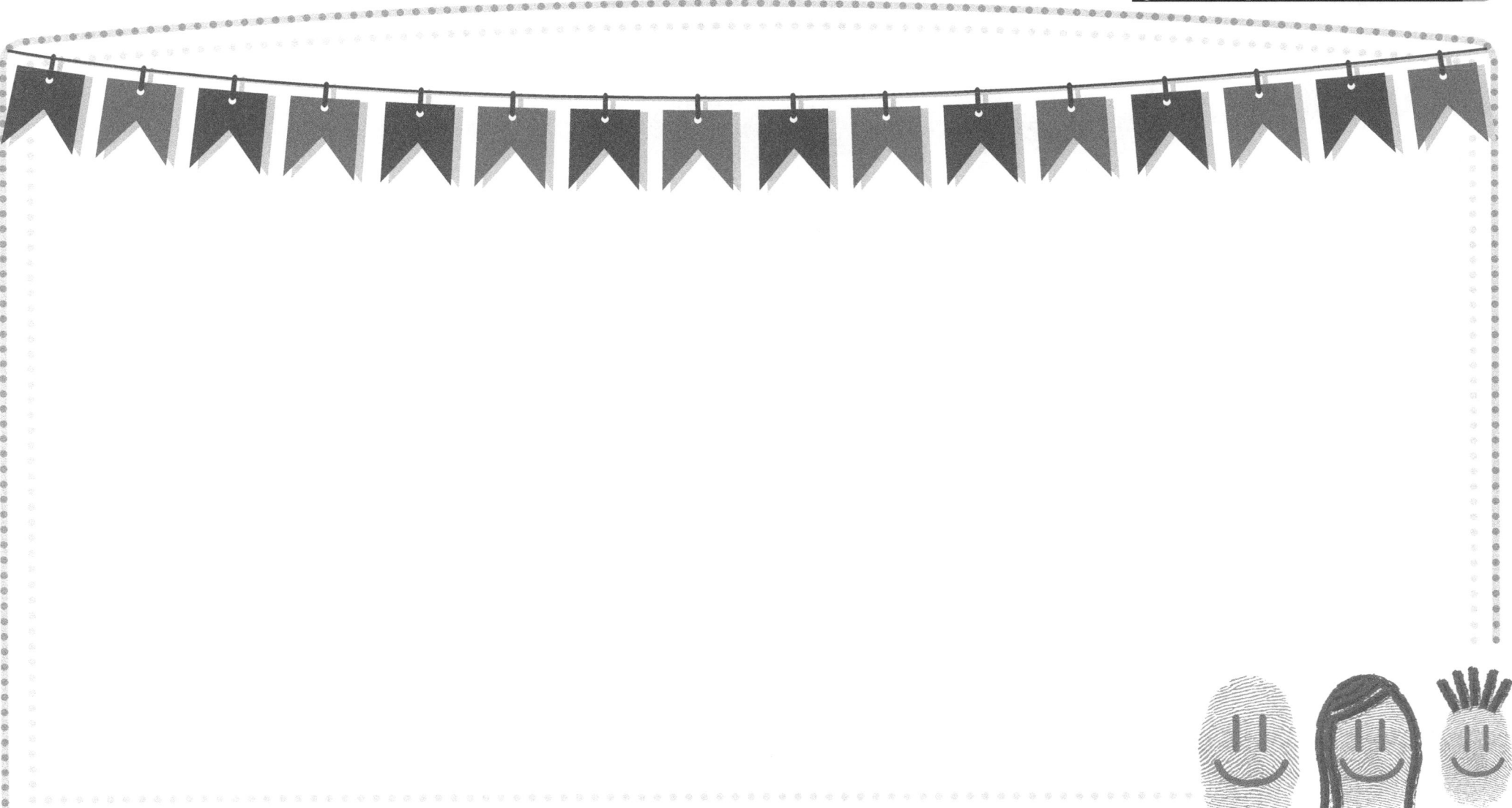

- **Talk about your drawing.**

Objectives: Create through drawing, painting, and modeling.

Artistic Expression and Appreciation
Learning to Be

Unit 3

- **Check who is helping.** ✓

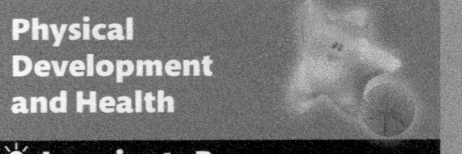

- **How can the other children help? Draw a picture.**

58 Unit 3

Objectives: Understand the importance of helping and being responsible.

- **Circle the objects that begin with the letter T t.**

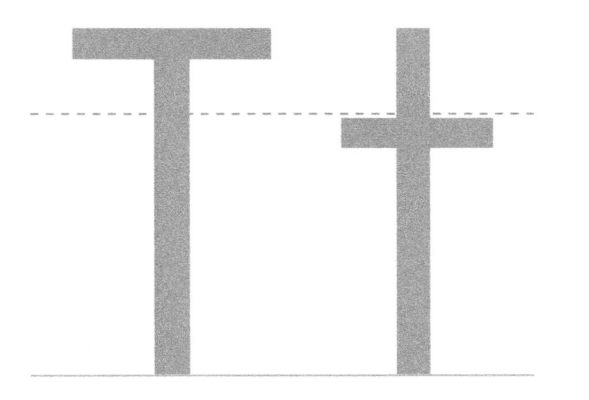

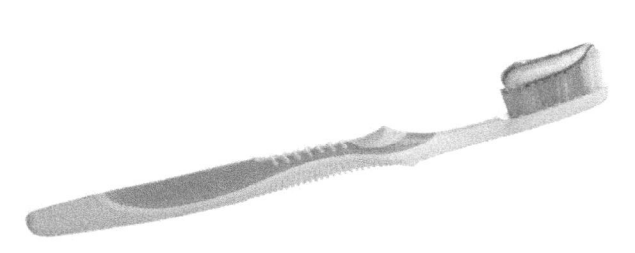

Tt

Objectives: Identify the initial /t/ sound.

Unit 3

- **Look at the Class Calendar. Write the date. Write the numbers.**

Month: _____ Year: _____

Monday	Tuesday	Wednesday	Thursday	Friday	Saturday	Sunday

Mathematical Thinking
Learning to Know

- **Complete the words.**

toys   table

- **Read the sentence.**

A 🪑 full of 🧸.

Unit 3

- **Draw to complete the pictures.**

Artistic Expression and Appreciation
Learning to Be

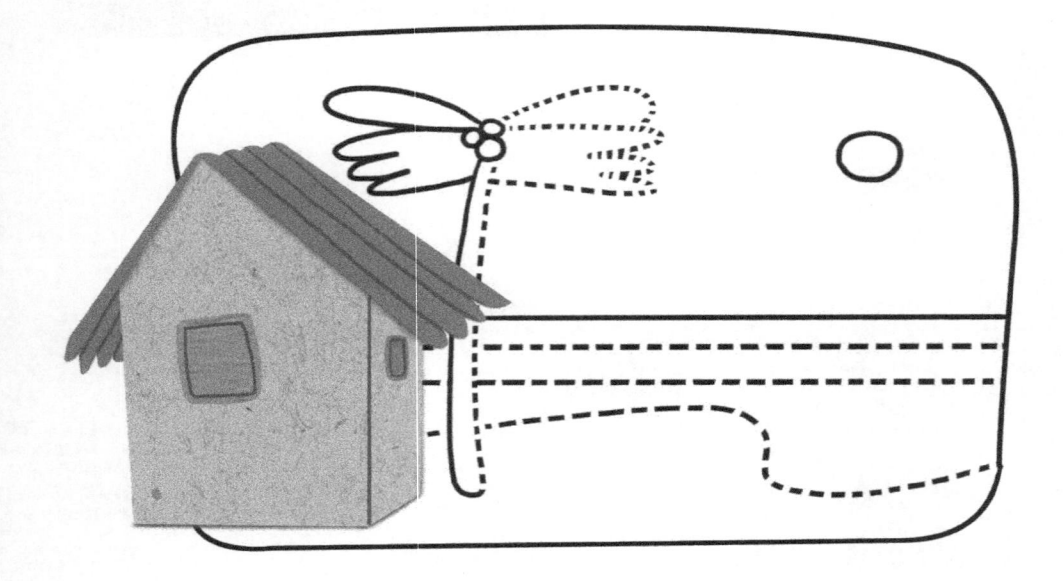

This house is by the sea.

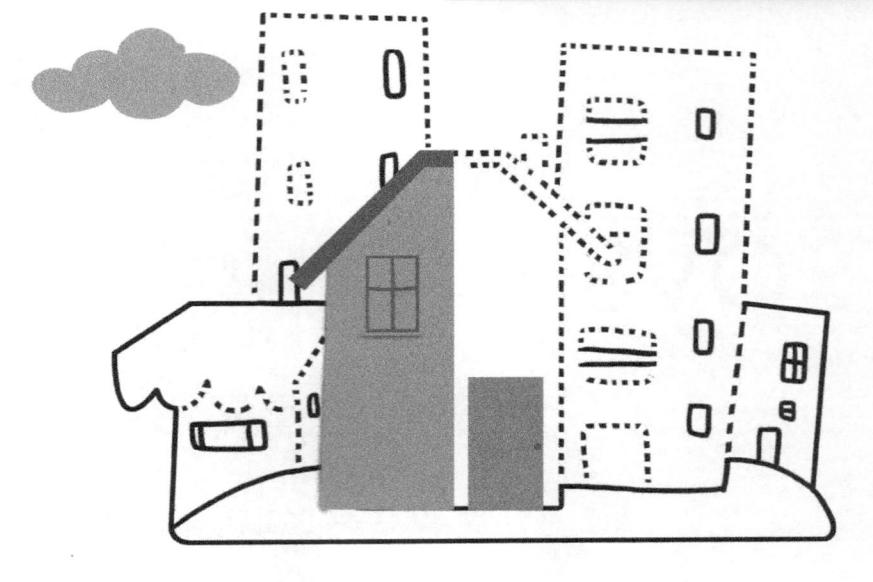

This house is in the city.

This house is on a mountain.

This house is on wheels.

Unit 3

Objectives: Create through drawing, painting, and modeling.

- **Circle the dangerous thing to do.**

- **Color the picture where the children are playing safely.**

Unit 3

Objectives: Be safe at home.

Physical Development and Health

Learning to Be

- **Match the letters to the words that start with *p*.**

Phonemic Awareness

Learning to Know

Pp

64 Unit 4

Objectives: Identify the initial /p/ sound.

• **Point and say. Trace and write.**

Mathematical Thinking

Learning to Know

1	2	3	4	5
6	7	8	9	10
	12		14	
16	17		19	20
21		23	24	25
	27	28		30

Objectives: Rote count to 30. Trace over numbers and write missing numbers.

● Look and say. Then write.

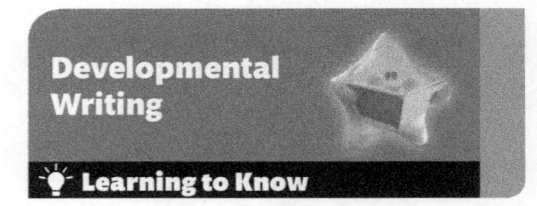

Developmental Writing

Learning to Know

Pp

Listen to the rain: pitter patter, pitter patter, pitter patter.

- **Look and say what you see in each picture.**

Artistic Expression and Appreciation
Learning to Be

- **Now finish the pictures.**

Objectives: Complete a drawing related to the weather.

Unit 4

- **Talk about the weather in each picture. Then match the objects to the child that needs them.**

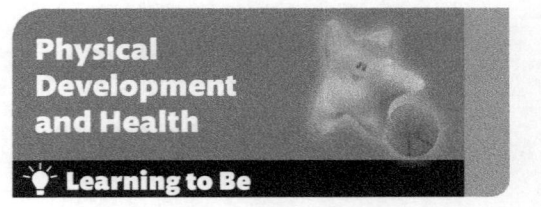

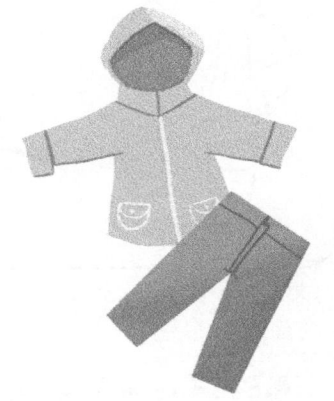

Physical Development and Health
Learning to Be

Objectives: Notice similarities and differences among people, places, events, and objects.

- **Pack your bag with things that start with p.**

Phonemic Awareness
Learning to Know

Objectives: Identify the initial /p/ sound.

Unit 4

● **Look and extend the patterns.**

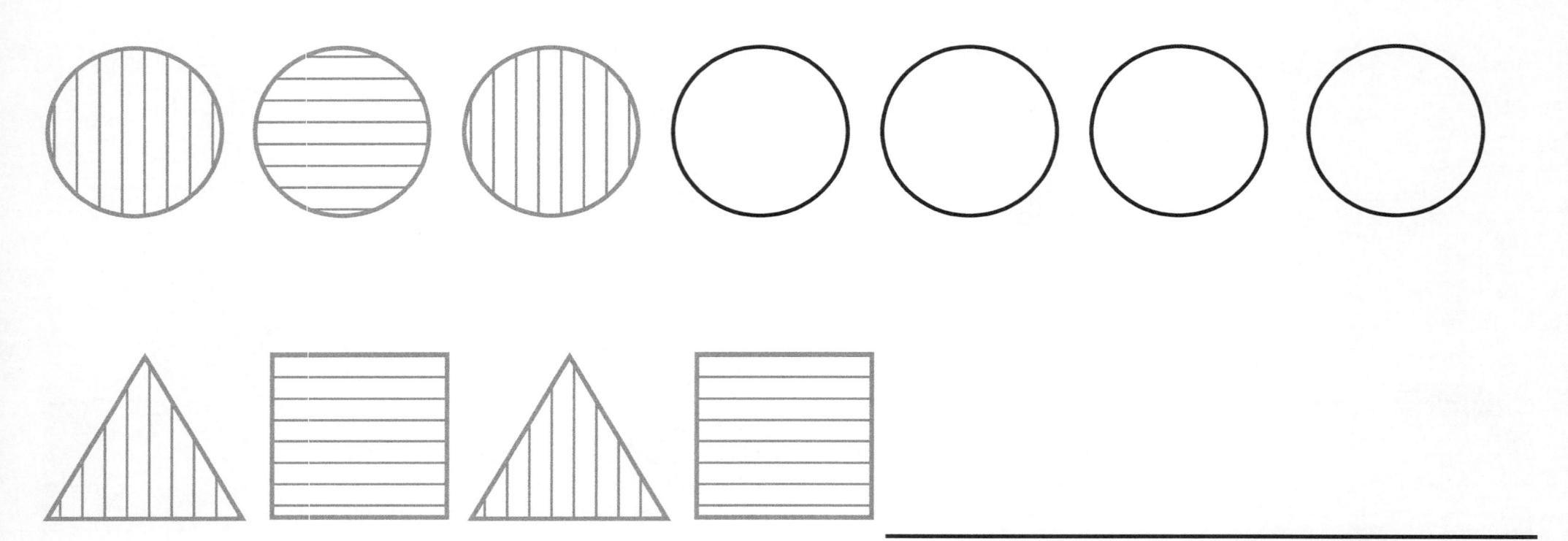

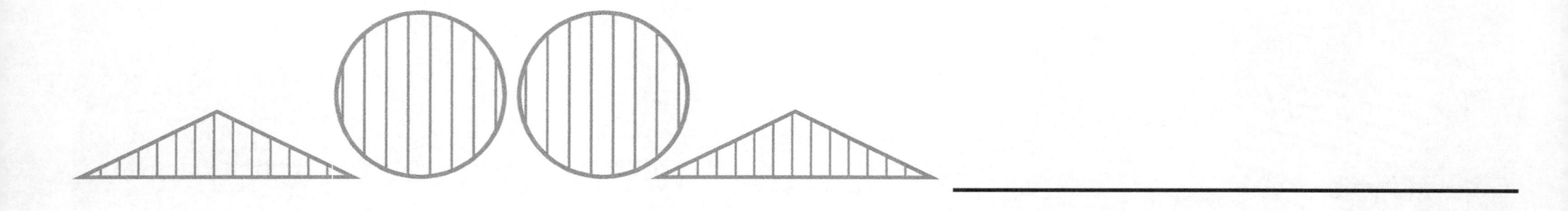

Mathematical Thinking

Learning to Know

70 Unit 4

Objectives: Can extend more complex patterns.

- **What is the boy wearing?**

- **Write the sentence.**

My pants are pajamas.
My pajamas are pants.

Objectives: Trace letter p.

Unit 4

- **Match the best clothes for each weather.**

Artistic Expression and Appreciation

Learning to Be

Unit 4

Objectives: Choose clothing for different types of weather.

- **Complete the umbrella.**

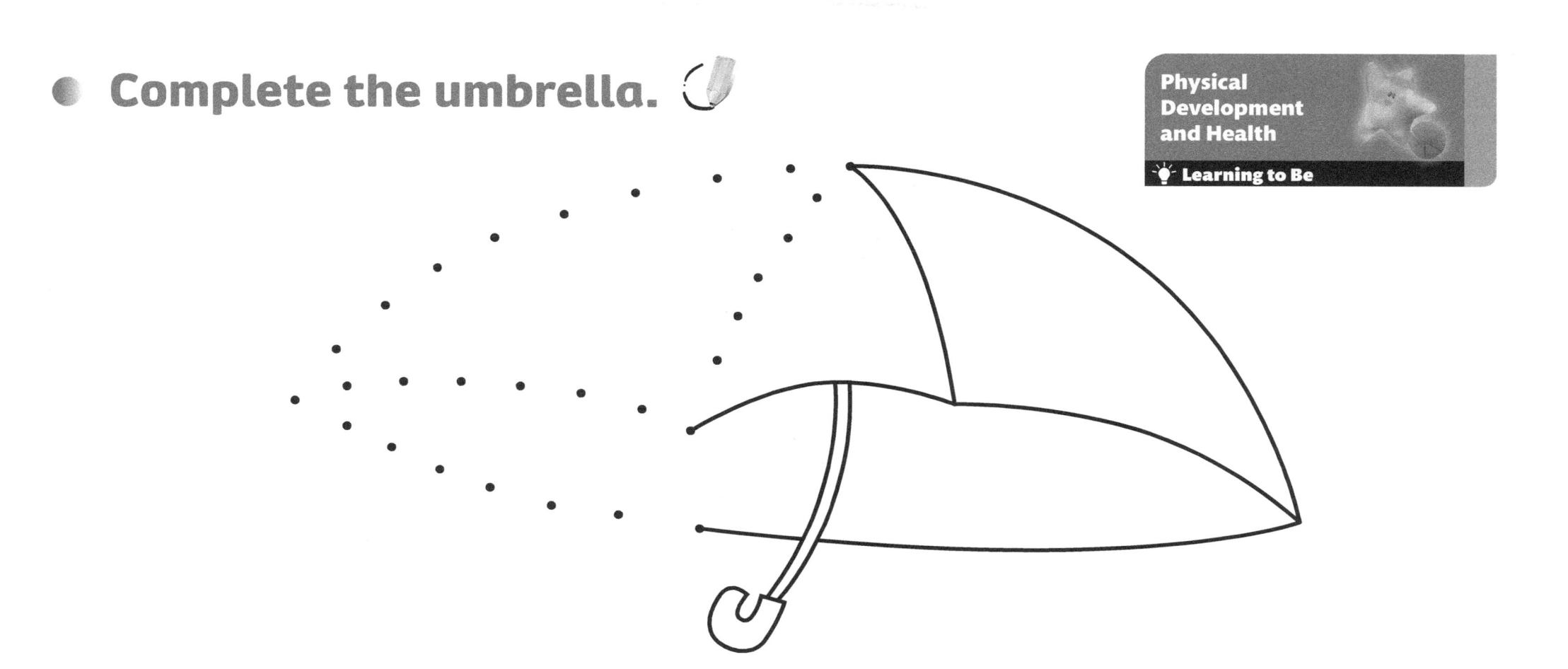

You can share my umbrella!

- **Draw yourself under the umbrella.**

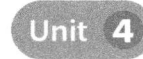

Physical Development and Health
Learning to Be

Objectives: Talk about what people should do to protect themselves in different types of weather.

Match the sound for each word.

Cc

74 Unit 4

Objectives: Identify the initial /c/ sound.

- **Color a square for each item you have.**

  Mathematical Thinking

  Learning to Know

  shoes

  jacket

  shorts

  shirt

  Objectives: Make a simple pictograph.

  Unit 4

- **Look and say. Then write.**

Cc

Cool cats like clouds.

- **Draw something that begins with C. Decorate the frame.**

Developmental Writing
Learning to Know

Objectives: Trace letter c.

- **Make a collage of your favorite weather.**

Artistic Expression and Appreciation
Learning to Be

Objectives: Make a collage of a type of weather and share it with the class.

Unit 4

- **Draw the weather yesterday and today.**

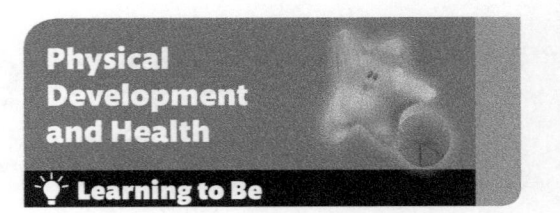

  yesterday | today

- **Mark the clothes you need to wear today.**

Physical Development and Health

Learning to Be

Unit 4

Objectives: Talk about what people should do to protect themselves in different types of weather.

- **Color the pictures that start with *n*.**

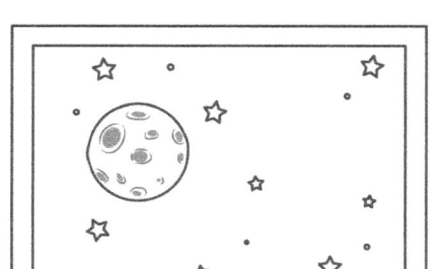

Phonemic Awareness

Learning to Know

Nn

Objectives: Identify the initial /n/ sound.

Unit 4

- **Look at the Class Calendar. Copy the month and the year. Copy the numbers.**

Month: _____ Year: _____

Monday	Tuesday	Wednesday	Thursday	Friday	Saturday	Sunday

- **Find out who has birthdays this month.**

Objectives: Identify and write numbers to 30. Say the date.

- **Look and say. What is the girl wearing? Then write.**

Norah has nine new hats.

- **Color the hot thermometer red and the cold thermometer blue.**

Artistic Expression and Appreciation

Learning to Be

82 Unit 4

Objectives: Identify different temperatures.

- **Draw yourself protecting from the sun.**

Physical Development and Health

Learning to Be

Objectives: Talk about protecting from sunny weather.

Unit 4

- **Circle in red the objects that start with *n*. Circle in green the objects that start with *p*.**

Phonemic Awareness

Learning to Know

Nn

Pp

84 Unit 4

Objectives: Identify initial /n/ and /p/ sounds.

- **Color the heavy object blue and the light object orange.**

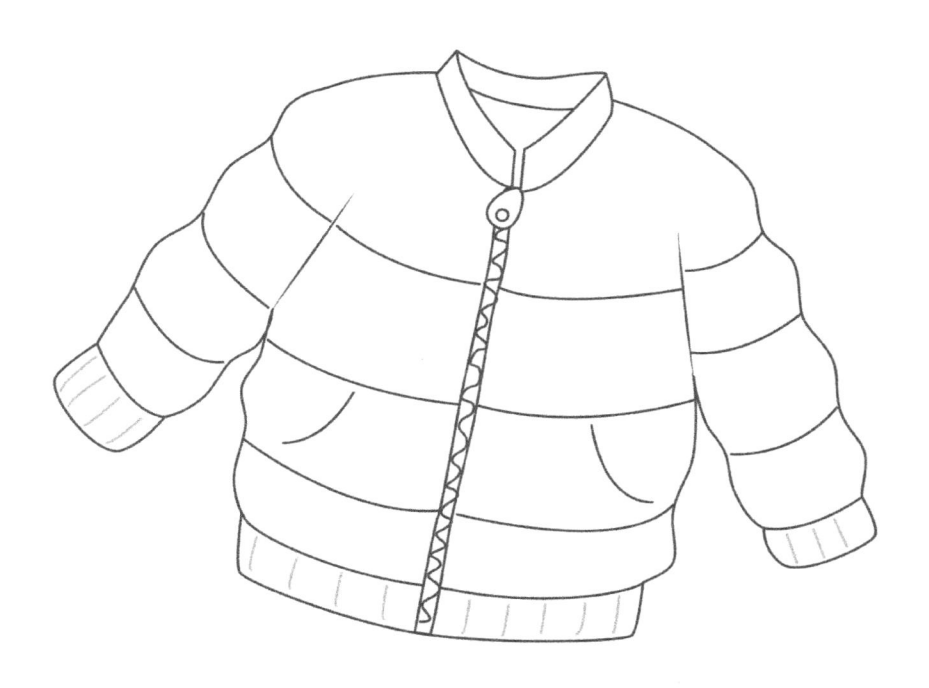

Mathematical Thinking

Learning to Know

Objectives: Distinguish between heavy and light.

Unit 4

- **Look and say. Then write.**

Nine penguins with nine pencils and nine notebooks.

Unit 4

Objectives: Trace letters *n* and *p*.

- **Paste a picture of the weather.**

Clothes I wear

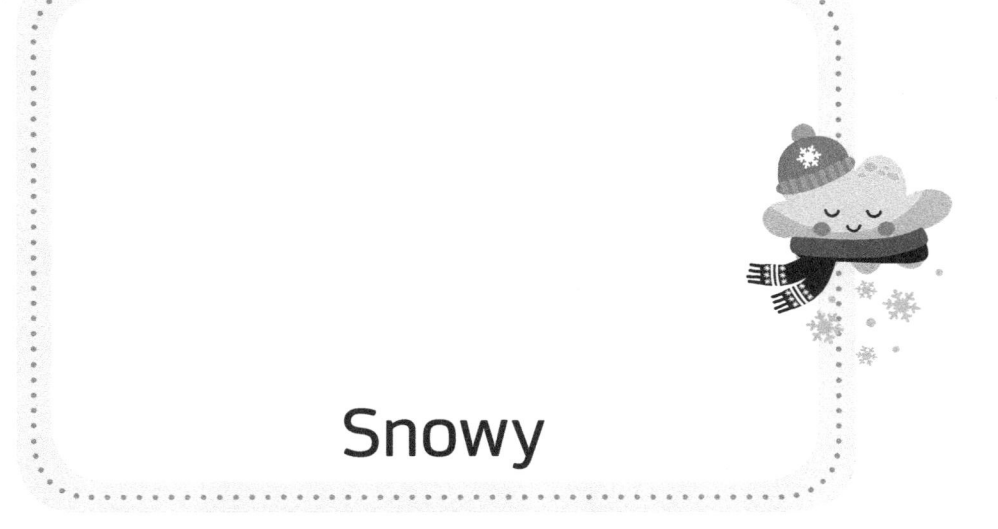

Sunny

Snowy

Rainy

Windy

- **Paste pictures of the clothes you wear in each weather.**

Artistic Expression and Appreciation
Learning to Be

Objectives: Identify and select appropriate clothes for different weathers.

Unit 4

- **Match the pictures.**

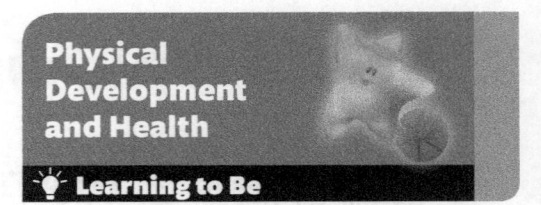

Physical Development and Health
Learning to Be

- **Color the pictures.**

Unit 4

Objectives: Reflect on what to do with old clothing.

- **Trace the letters. Color c, n or p.**

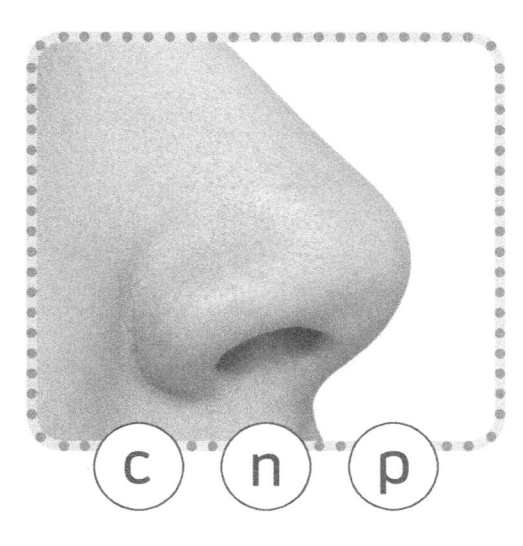

Cc Nn Pp

Phonemic Awareness

Learning to Know

c n p	c n p	c n p	c n p
c n p	c n p	c n p	c n p

Objectives: Identify initial /c/, /n/, and /p/ sounds.

Unit 4

Count. Write. Fingerpaint.

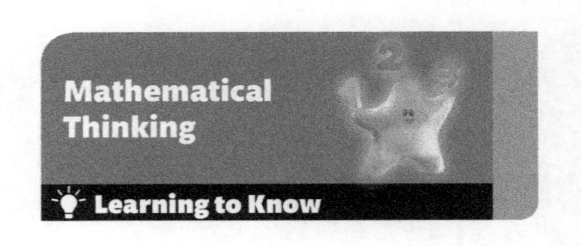

0 1 2 3 4 5 6 7 8 9 10 11 12 13 14 15 16 17 18 19 20

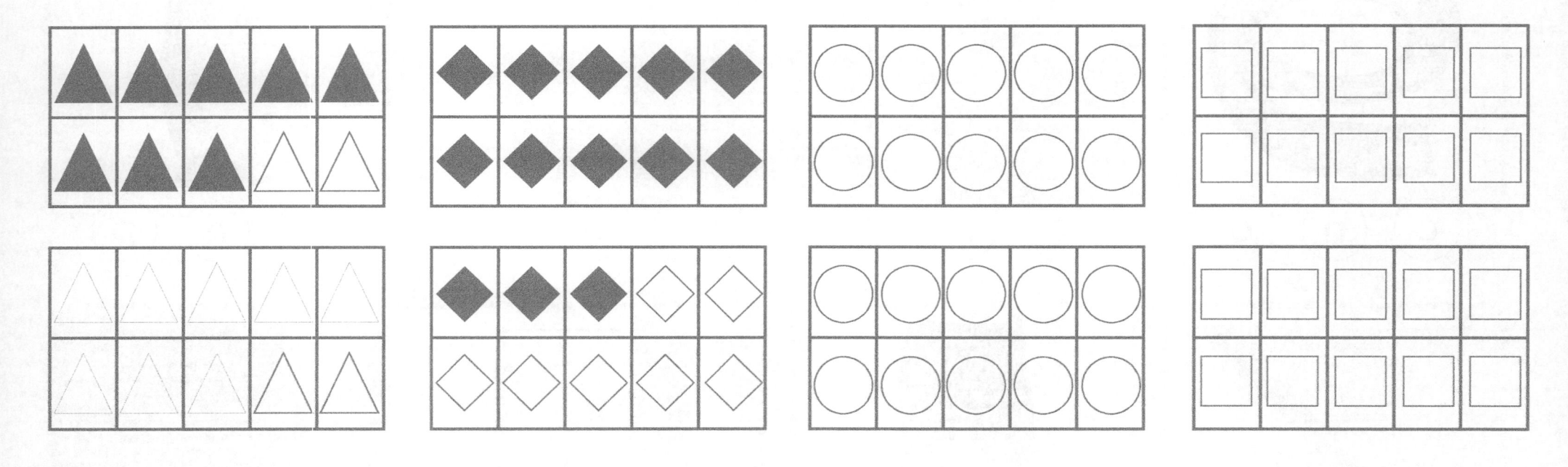

Mathematical Thinking
Learning to Know

8 _____   _____   18   20

Objectives: Count up to 20.

- **Look and say. Then write.**

Developmental Writing

Learning to Know

Nine cats with pants are under the cloud.

Objectives: Trace letters c, n, and p.

Unit 4

- **Talk about what the children are doing. Then complete the picture.**

Artistic Expression and Appreciation

Learning to Be

92 Unit 4

Objectives: Draw a scene.

- **Order the pictures.**

Physical Development and Health
Learning to Be

- **Act out.**

Objectives: Learn how to take care of ourselves in cases of cold and flu.

Unit 4

- **Check the pictures that star with *b*.** ✔

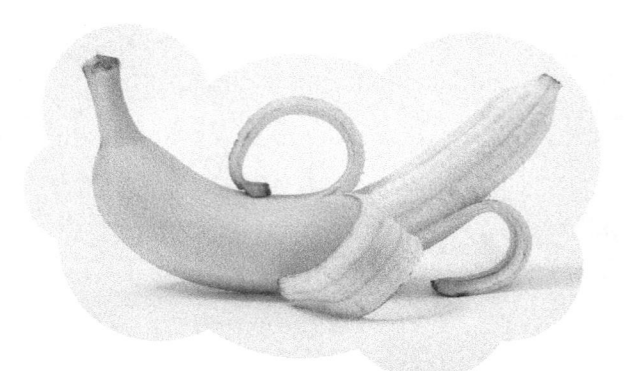

Phonemic Awareness
💡 Learning to Know

Bb

94 Unit 5

Objectives: Identify the initial /b/ sound.

● **Point, say, trace, and write.**

1	2	3	4		6		8	9	10
11		13		15	16	17	18	19	20
21	22		24		26	27		29	30
31	32	33	34		36		38	39	40
41		43		45	46	47	48		50

Mathematical Thinking

 Learning to Know

Objectives: Rote count to 50. Trace over numbers and write missing numbers. Begin to count by 10's.

Unit 5

Look and say. Then write.

A busy, busy butterfly and a buzzing, buzzing bee.

- **Make an insect collage.**

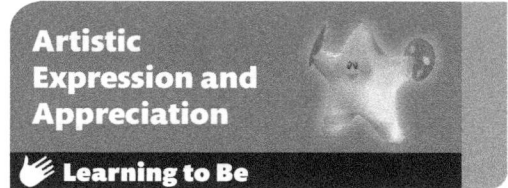

- **Share your pictures. Prepare an art exhibition.**

Artistic Expression and Appreciation

Learning to Be

Objectives: Make an insect collage and find similarities and differences.

Unit 5

- **Name all the insects. Then color your favorite insect.**

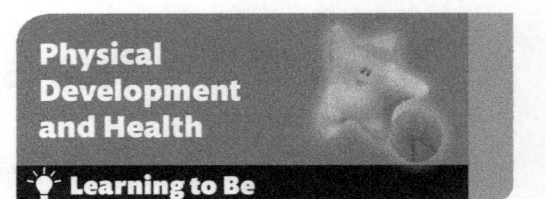

Physical Development and Health
Learning to Be

98 Unit 5

Objectives: Identify living things. Express likes and dislikes.

- **Match the letters to the words that start with f.**

Phonemic Awareness

Learning to Know

Ff

Objectives: Identify the initial /f/ sound.

Unit 5

- **Look, say, and extend the patterns.**

  Mathematical Thinking
  Learning to Know

  1. A A B A A B _ _ _ _ _ _

  2. C A X C A X _ _ _ _ _ _

  3. 🌼 🌿 _ _ _ _ _ _

  4. 🦋 🐝 _ _ _ _ _ _

Objectives: Extend more complex patterns.

- **Look and say. Then write.**

Developmental Writing
Learning to Know

Flowers and fruit have fun in the sun.

Objectives: Trace letter f.

- **Fingerpaint the butterfly.**

Artistic Expression and Appreciation
Learning to Be

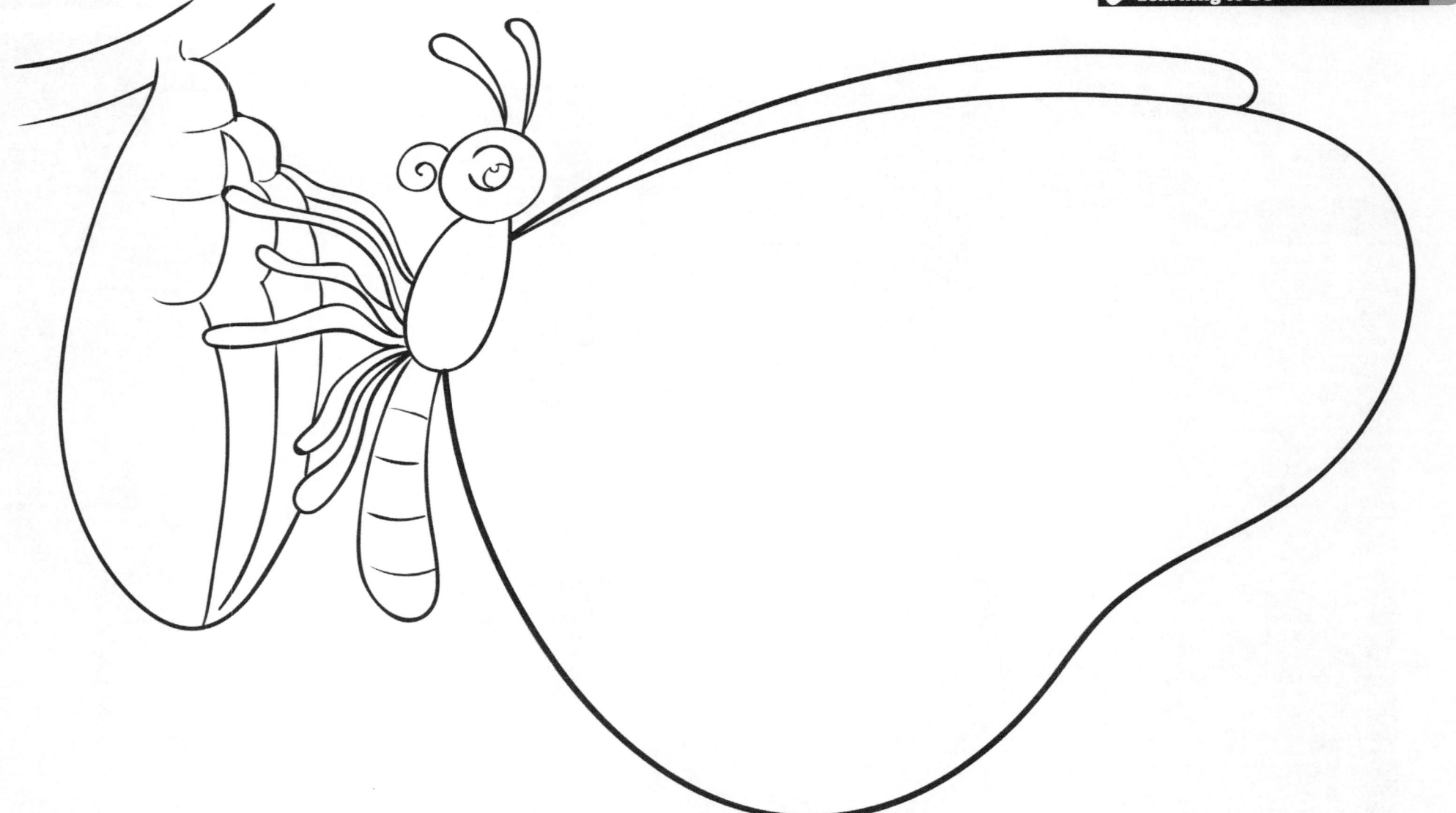

- **How many colors are there in your butterfly?**

Objectives: Fingerpaint a butterfly.

- **Help the bee travel from one flower to the other.**

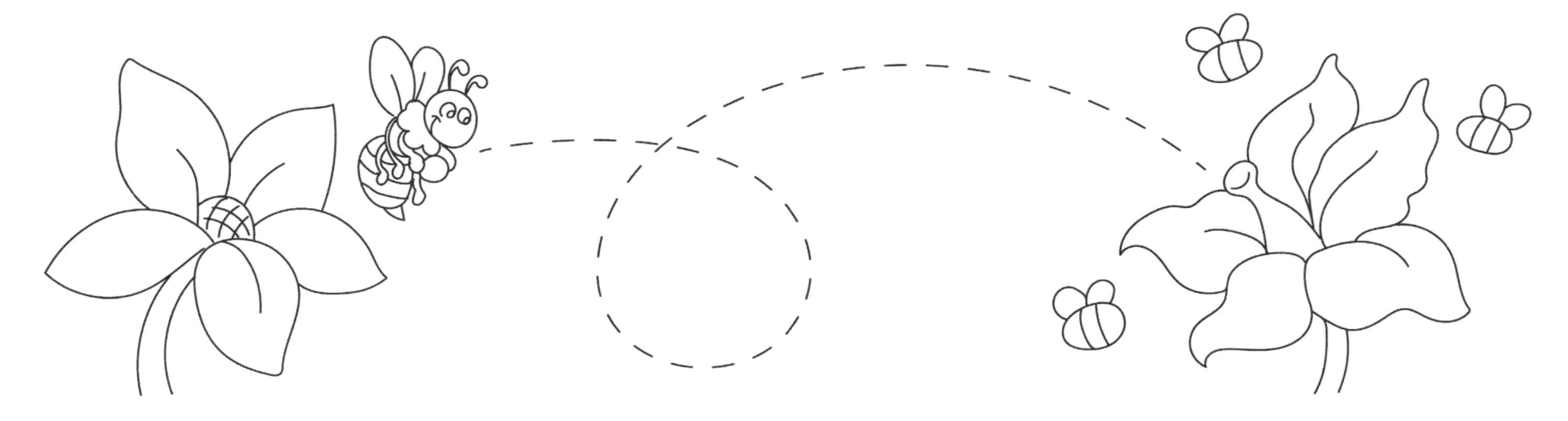

- **The flowers need bees. Draw the bees.**

Physical Development and Health
Learning to Be

Objectives: Respect plants and insects.

Unit 5   103

● **Circle the objects that start with *r*.**

Phonemic Awareness
Learning to Know

Rr

104 Unit 5

Objectives: Identify the initial /r/ sound.

- **Color the triangles green. Color the rectangles purple. Color the rhombuses yellow.**

Mathematical Thinking

Learning to Know

- **Look and say. Then write.**

Developmental Writing
- Learning to Know

The robot wears rings in the rain.

106 Unit 5

Objectives: Trace letter r.

- **How many leaves can you find? Paste the leaves into the chart.**

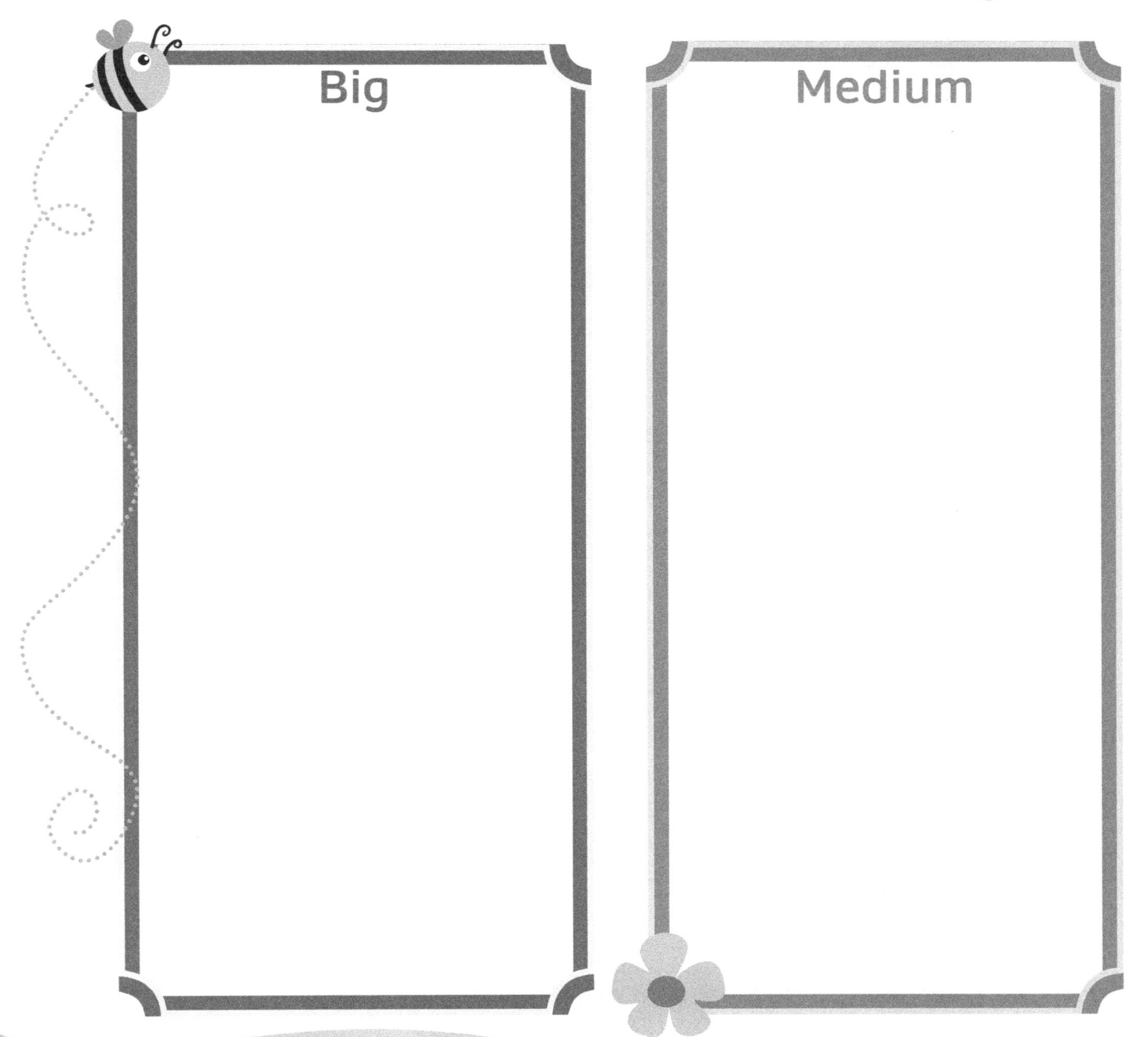

Big	Medium	Small

Artistic Expression and Appreciation

Learning to Be

Objectives: Collect samples of leaves and seeds.

Unit 5

- **Draw happy faces on the flowers.**

- **Talk about one of the flowers. Why are they happy or sad?**

Physical Development and Health

Learning to Be

Objectives: Recognize and talk about feelings.

- **Color the initial letter in each word.**

Phonemic Awareness

Learning to Know

(b) (f) (r)   (b) (f) (r)   (b) (f) (r)

(b) (f) (r)   (b) (f) (r)   (b) (f) (r)

Objectives: Identify initial /b/, /f/, and /r/ sounds.

- **Look at the Class Calendar. Copy the month and year. Copy number 1 on the first month.**

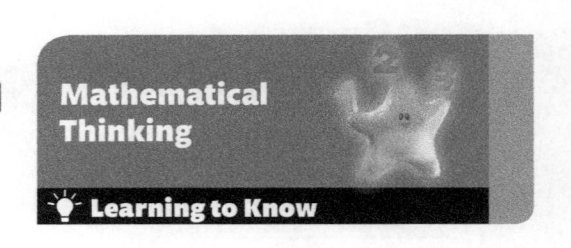

Mathematical Thinking
Learning to Know

| April | June | August | October | December | February |
| May | July | September | November | January | March |

Month: _____ Year: _____

| Monday | Tuesday | Wednesday | Thursday | Friday | Saturday | Sunday |

- **Look and say. Then write.**

The boy loves the butterfly. The butterfly loves the flowers. The flowers love the rain.

- **Fingerpaint a nature scene.**

Artistic Expression and Appreciation
Learning to Be

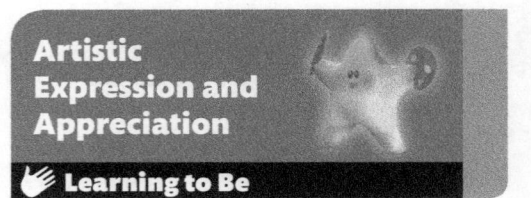

- **Share with a partner. Compare your pictures.**

112 Unit 5

Objectives: Compare similarities and differences.

- ## Check the pictures of pets. ✓

Physical Development and Health
Learning to Be

Objectives: Respect insects.

Unit 5 — 113

- **Match the letters to the words that start with *g*.**

Phonemic Awareness
Learning to Know

Gg

114 Unit 6

Objectives: Identify the initial /g/ sound.

- **Point. Say, trace, and match.**

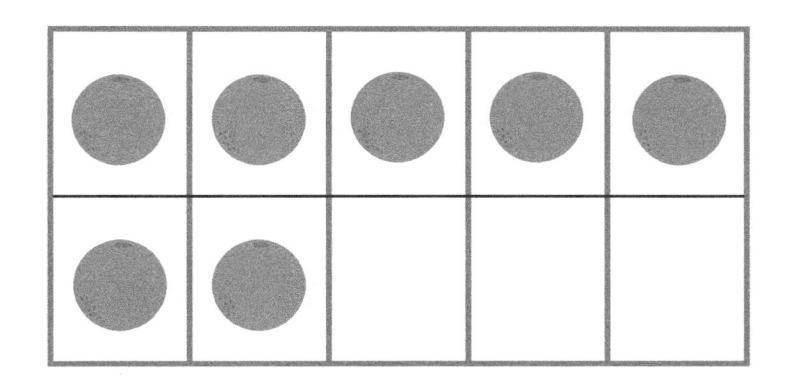

Mathematical Thinking
💡 Learning to Know

14
fourteen

7
seven

3
three

18
eighteen

9
nine

Objectives: Match numbers and objects.

Unit 6 **115**

- **Look and say. Then write.**

Developmental Writing

Learning to Know

Goats and gorillas love good grapes!

- **Match the food that is similar.**

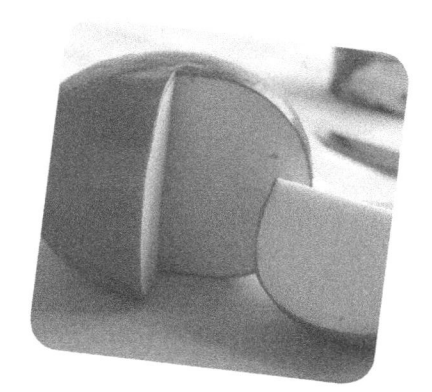

- **Draw the food you like the most.**

Artistic Expression and Appreciation

Learning to Be

Objectives: Identify similar food. Express preferences.

Unit 6 117

- **Draw the food you like to eat in the morning and in the evening.**

Physical Development and Health
Learning to Be

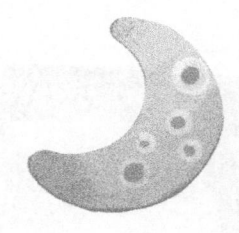

118 Unit 6

Objectives: Recognize which food they eat in the mornings and in the evenings. Express preferences.

- **Match the letters to the words that start with *h*.**

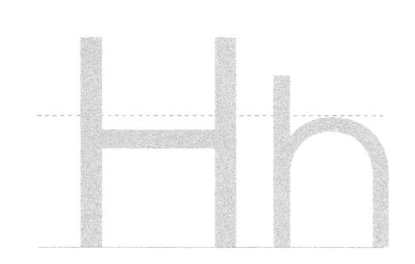

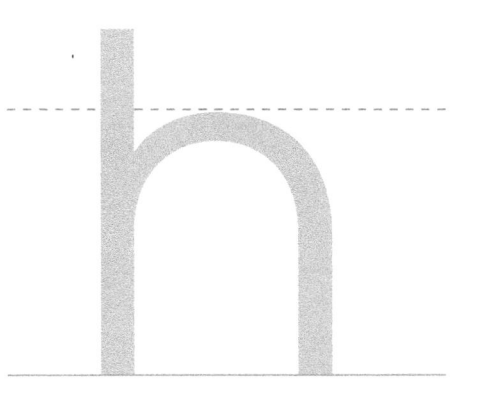

Phonemic Awareness

Learning to Know

Hh

h

Objectives: Identify the initial /h/ sound.

Unit 6 — 119

- **Color the objects that are smaller.**

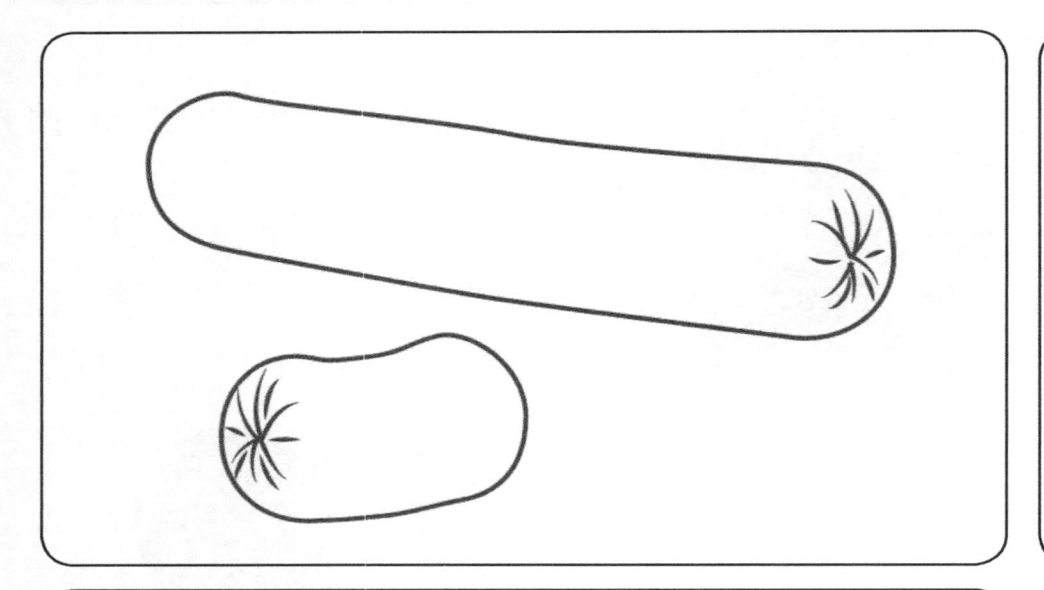

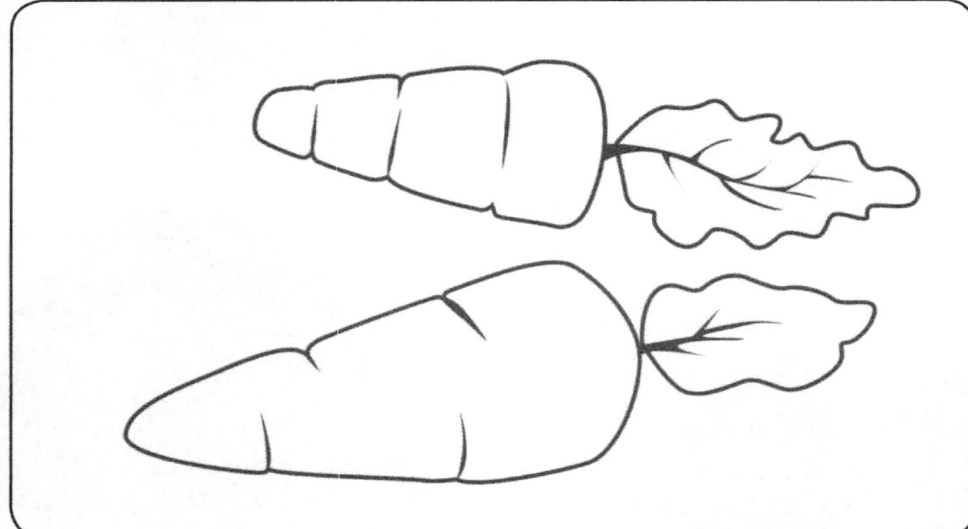

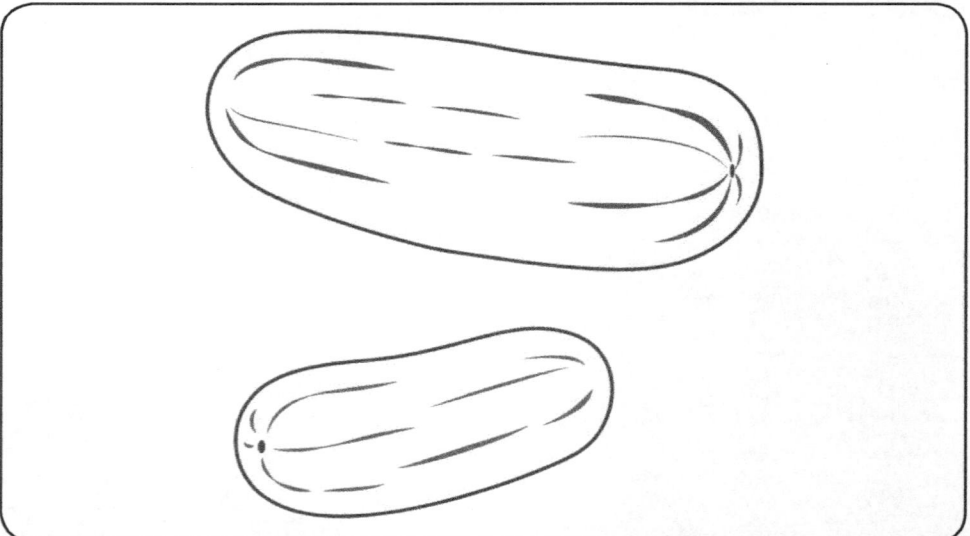

Mathematical Thinking

Learning to Know

- **Say the name of the food.**

120 Unit 6

Objectives: Identify longer and shorter objects.

- **Look and say. Then write.**

Developmental Writing

Learning to Know

Hh

Happy hungry hippos.

Unit 6

- **Draw what you eat for breakfast.**
  Draw what you eat for lunch.

Artistic Expression and Appreciation
Learning to Be

122 Unit 6

Objectives: Relate food or mealtimes to times of the day.

- **Number the pictures in order.**

Physical Development and Health
Learning to Be

Objectives: Develop social awareness of oneself and objects.

Unit 6 — 123

- **Color the words that start with *j*.**

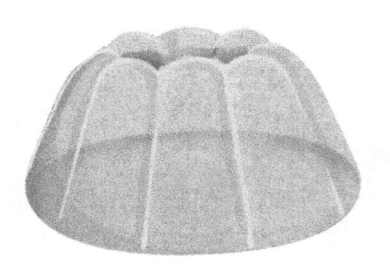

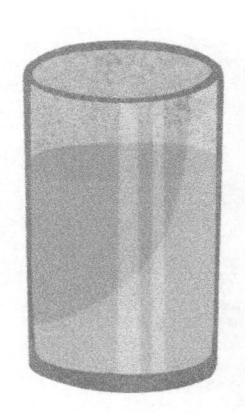

Phonemic Awareness

Learning to Know

Jj

Unit 6

Objectives: Identify the initial /j/ sound.

Complete the pattern. Color.

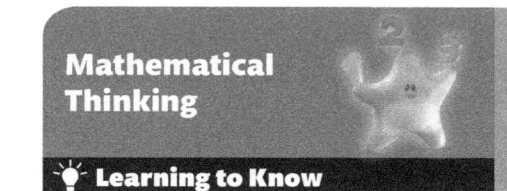

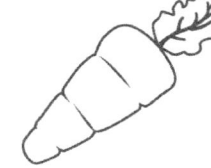

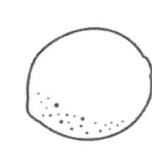

Mathematical Thinking

Learning to Know

Objectives: Extend patterns.

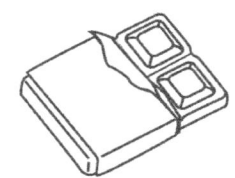

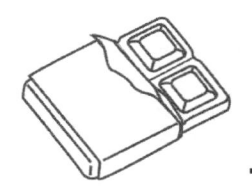

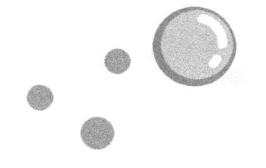

Unit 6 — 125

- **Look and say. Then write.**

I jump for jello and juice.

- **Complete the lunchbox and draw in healthy food.**

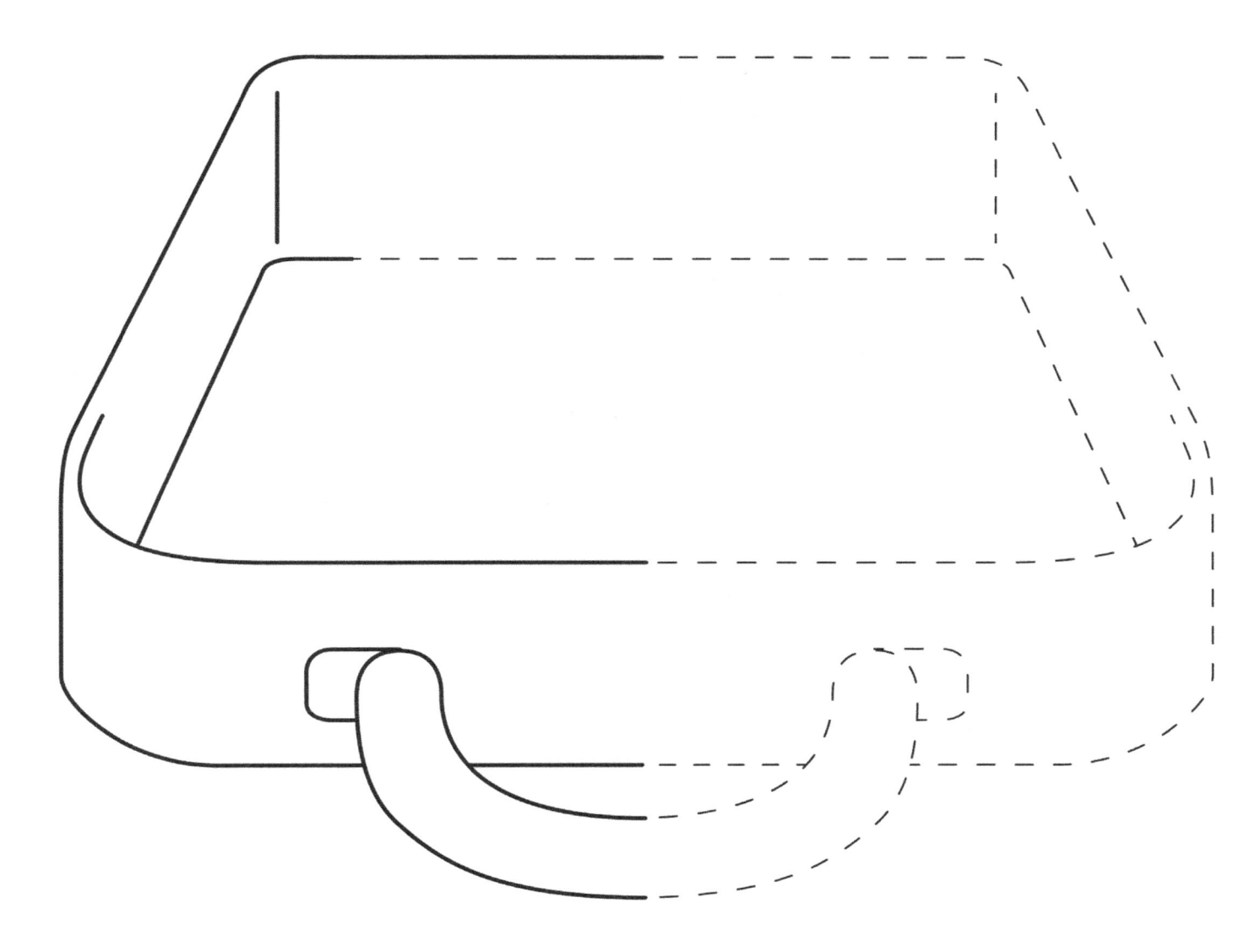

- **Name the foods.**

Objectives: Draw and fingerpaint healthy food.

Unit 6

- **Circle the healthy foods. Cross out the unhealthy foods.**

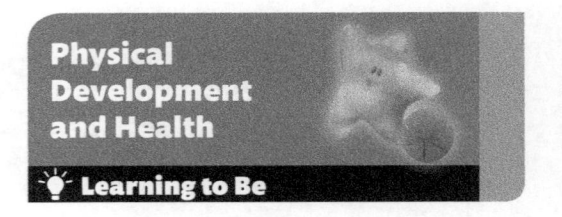

Physical Development and Health
Learning to Be

- **Say which food you ate today.**

Unit 6

Objectives: Identify healthy and unhealthy food/snacks.

- **Check the words that start with *k*.** ✓

Phonemic Awareness

Learning to Know

K k

Objectives: Identify the initial /k/ sound.

Unit 6   **129**

● Trace numbers and draw food.

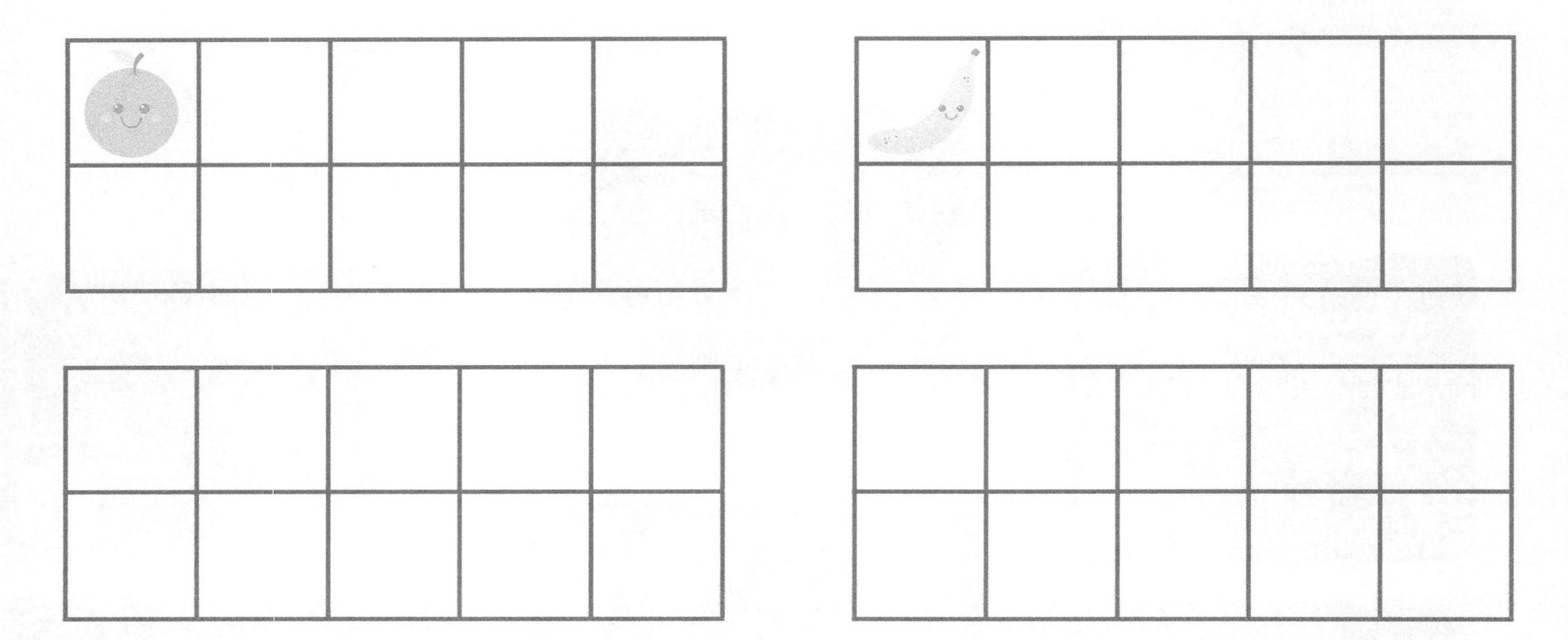

Mathematical Thinking
Learning to Know

18 oranges

16 bananas

● **Look and say. Then write.**

The kitten and the kangaroo play with the kites.

Objectives: Trace letter *k*.

- **Look at the sandwich. Is it healthy or unhealthy?**

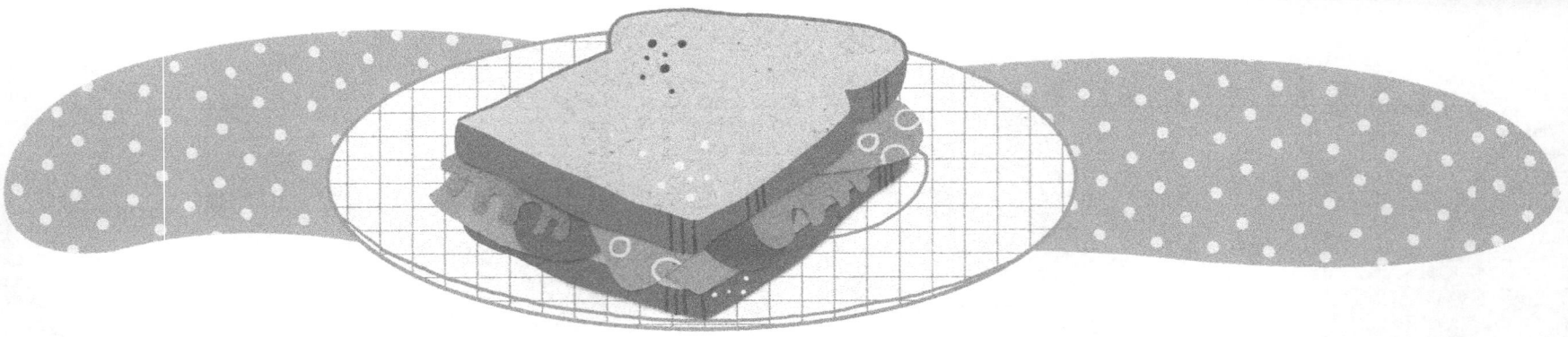

- **Make your sandwich. Paste or draw pictures of the ingredients.**

"My healthy sandwich"

Artistic Expression and Appreciation
Learning to Be

Objectives: Draw ingredients for a healthy snack.

- # Number the pictures.

Physical Development and Health

Learning to Be

- # Now make your sandwich.

Objectives: Order the steps to make a healthy snack.

Unit 6

- **Match the objects to the *g* or *h*.**

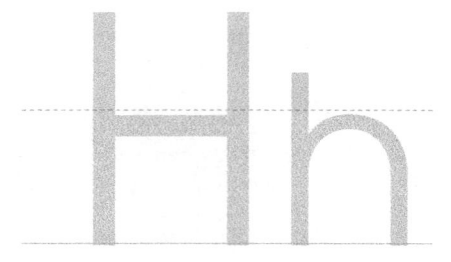

Gg

Hh

Phonemic Awareness

Learning to Know

134 Unit 6

Objectives: Identify initial /g/ and /h/ sounds.

- **Make a pictogram.**

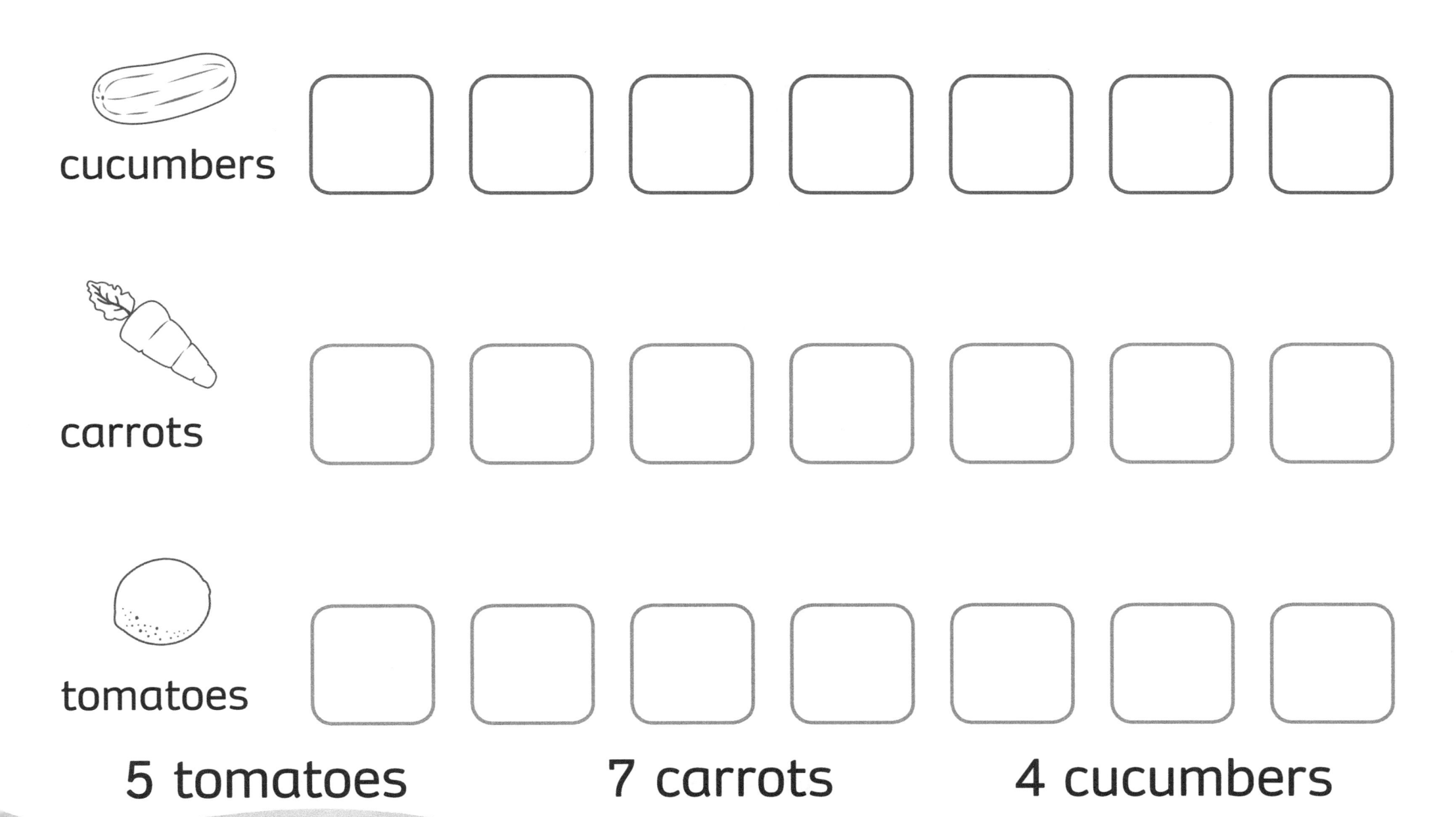

Mathematical Thinking
Learning to Know

cucumbers

carrots

tomatoes

5 tomatoes   7 carrots   4 cucumbers

Objectives: Make a simple pictogram.

Unit 6 — 135

● **Look and say. Then write.**

Developmental Writing
Learning to Know

Grandma's up high in a helicopter.

136 Unit 6

Objectives: Trace letters *g* and *h*.

- **Make a collage with food from your country.**

Artistic Expression and Appreciation

Learning to Be

Objectives: Identify food from own country.

Unit 6

- **Color the fruit.**

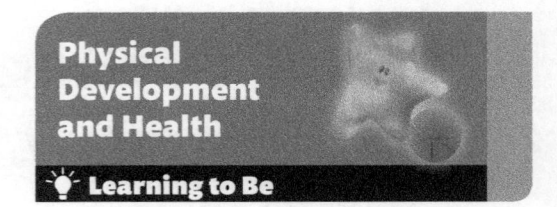

Physical Development and Health

Learning to Be

- **Number the pictures in order. What happens when we wash fruit?**

138 Unit 6

Objectives: Understand why we should wash vegetables and fruit before eating them.

- **Circle the beginning sound.**

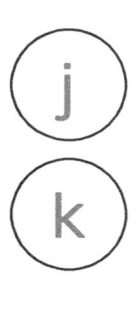

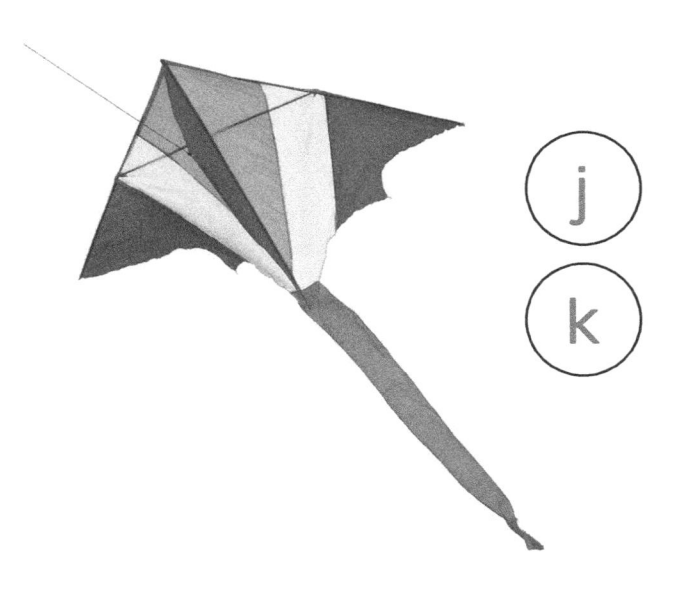

Phonemic Awareness

Learning to Know

Objectives: Identify initial /j/ and /k/ sounds.

Unit 6

- **Look at the Class Calendar. Copy the month and the year. Copy number 1.**

April	June	August	October	December	February
May	July	September	November	January	March

Month: _____ Year: _____

Monday	Tuesday	Wednesday	Thursday	Friday	Saturday	Sunday

Objectives: Identify and write numbers to 30. Say the date.

- **Look and say. Then write.**

Developmental Writing

Learning to Know

The jellyfish and the kangaroo like juice.

Objectives: Trace letters *j* and *k*.

Unit 6

- **Fingerpaint the fruit.**

- **Write the first letter of each fruit.**

142 Unit 6

Objectives: Color fruit.

- **Match the waste to the correct bin.**

Objectives: Classify organic and inorganic products.

Unit 6 — 143

- **Check the initial letter of the words.** ✓

Phonemic Awareness

💡 Learning to Know

W w

A ☐
W ☐

W ☐
B ☐

B ☐
W ☐

W ☐
A ☐

C ☐
W ☐

W ☐
B ☐

- **Color de objects that start with w.**

144 Unit 7

Objectives: Identify initial letter of the words.

- **Skip count by 10's. Trace in blue.**
  Skip count by 5's. Trace in green.

Mathematical Thinking
Learning to Know

1	2	3	4	5	6	7	8	9	10
11	12	13	14	15	16	17	18	19	20
21	22	23	24	25	26	27	28	29	30
31	32	33	34	35	36	37	38	39	40
41	42	43	44	45	46	47	48	49	50

Objectives: Skip count by 10's and begin to skip count by 5's.

- **Look and say. Then write.**

The worm and the whale try to whistle.

- **Draw a picture that starts with w.**

- **Find the animals. Then color them.**

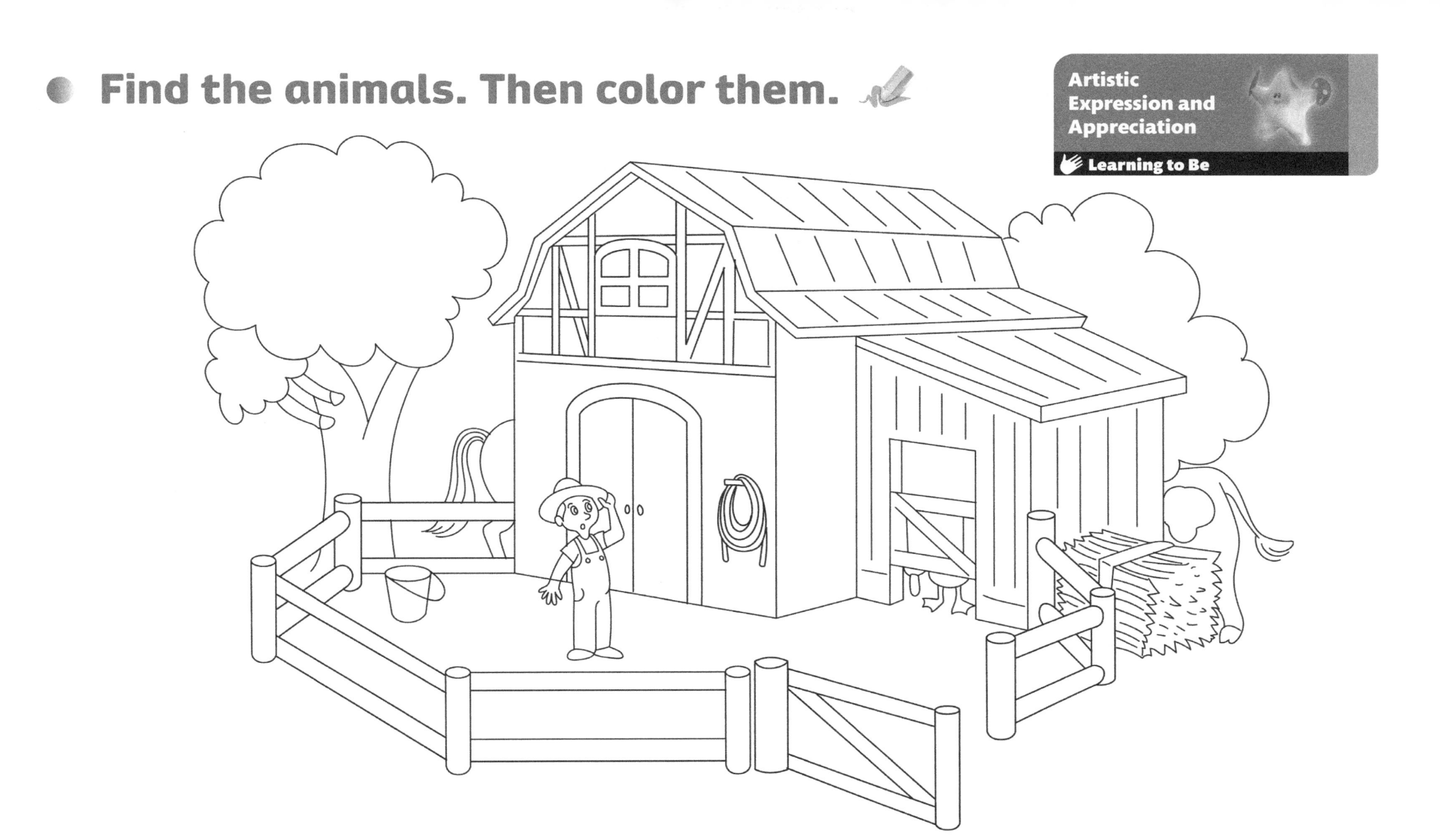

- **Where can you find these animals? Circle.**

At school. On a farm.

Objectives: Identify farm animals.

Unit 7

- **Choose and draw an animal.**

Physical Development and Health
Learning to Be

- **Find out about your animal. Have a class exhibition.**

Unit 7

Objectives: Learn more about farm animals.

- **Match the objects that start with *v*. Trace the letters.**

Vv

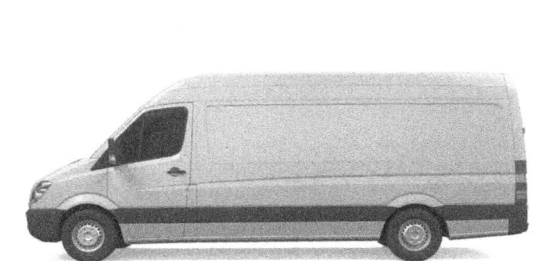

Objectives: Identify the initial /v/ sound.

Phonemic Awareness

Learning to Know

Unit 7

• **Complete the pattern.**

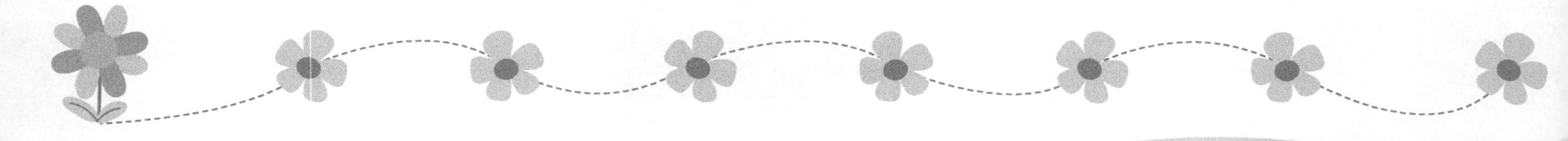

150   Unit 7

Objectives: Extend complex patterns.

● Look and say. Then write.

Violins don't wear vests!

● **Match the animals to their names.**

cow

sheep

hen

calf

lamb

chicken

● **Color the baby animals.**

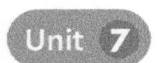

Artistic Expression and Appreciation
Learning to Be

- **Match the lamb to the things it needs.**

Physical Development and Health

Learning to Be

Objectives: Learn what animals need.

Unit 7 **153**

- **Follow the maze to connect the objects to the y.**

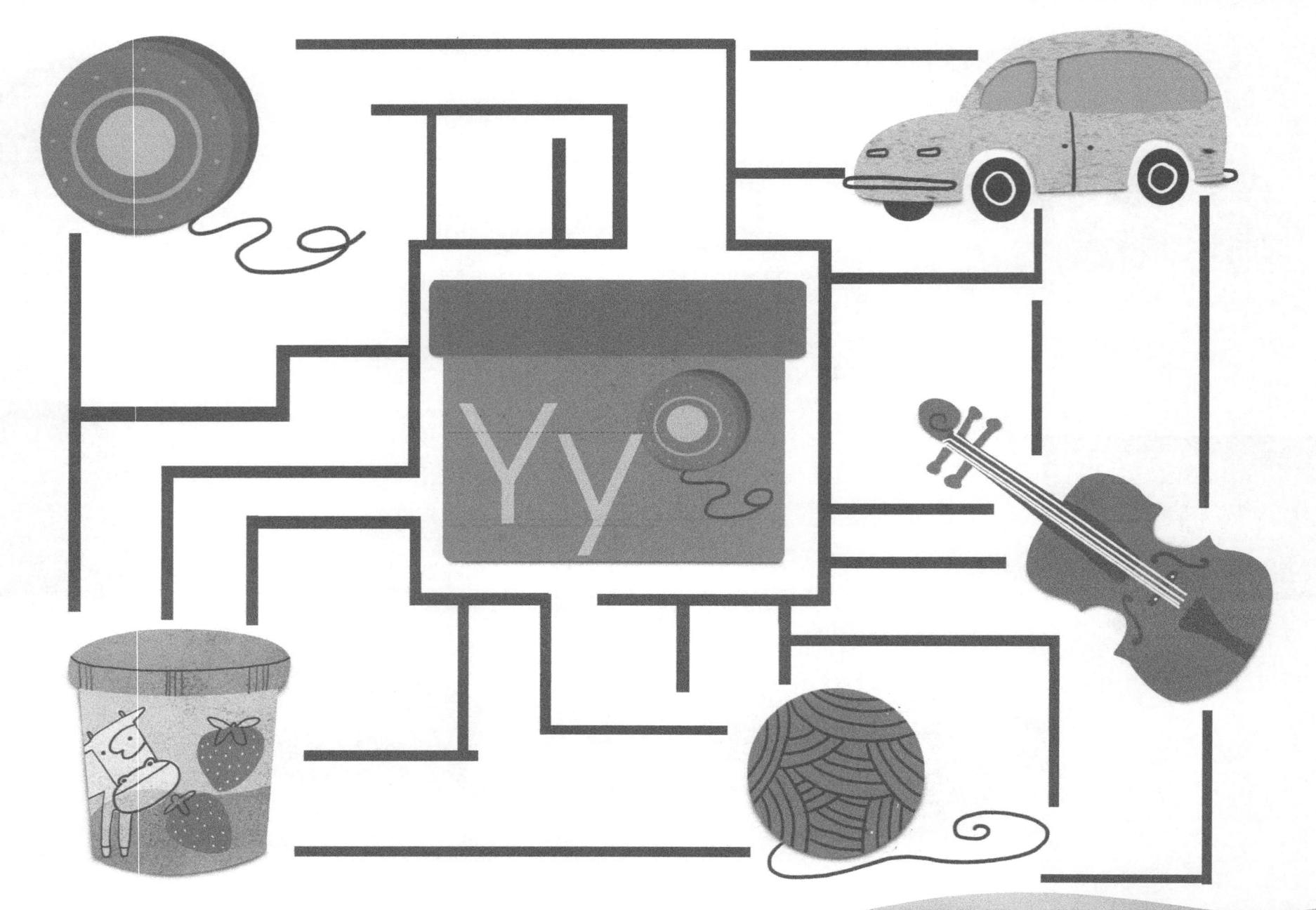

Phonemic Awareness
Learning to Know

154 Unit 7

Objectives: Identify the initial /y/ sound.

- **Listen and draw.**

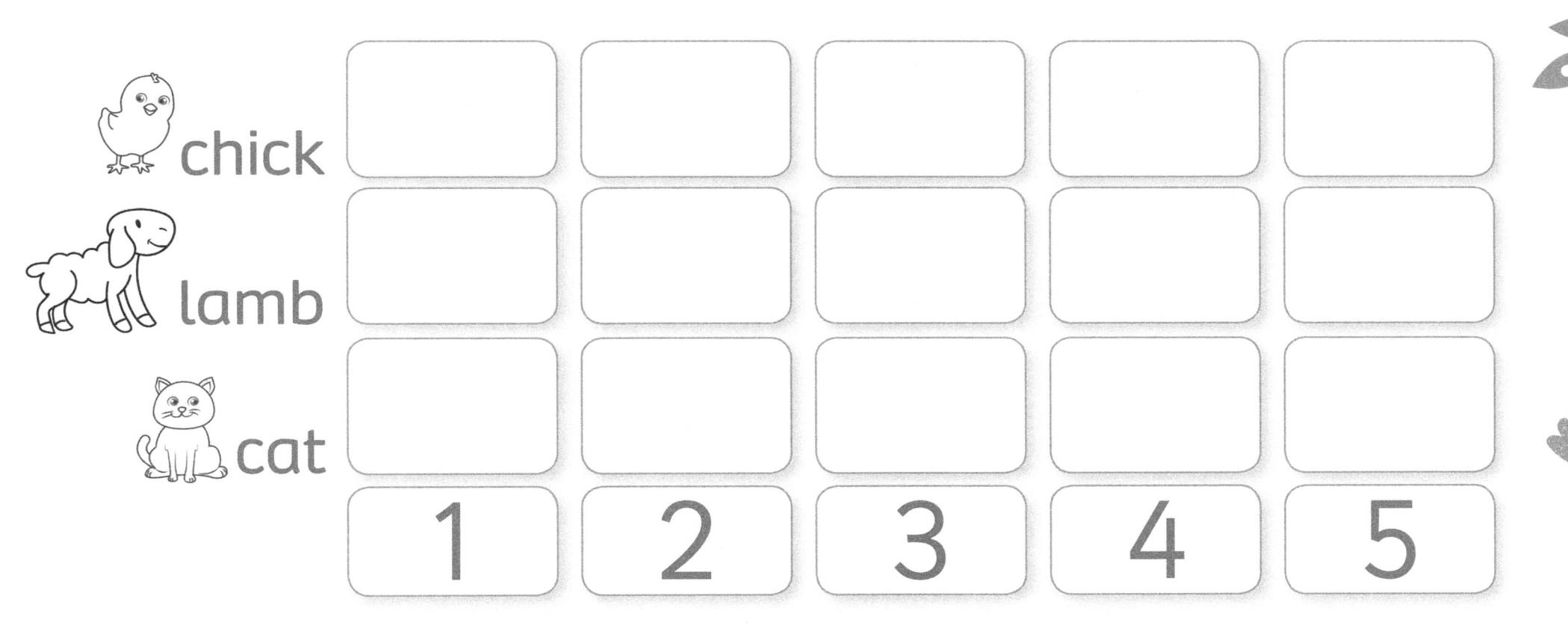

Mathematical Thinking
Learning to Know

	1	2	3	4	5
chick					
lamb					
cat					

There are 3 lambs.
There are 5 chicks.
There are 2 cats.

Objectives: Make a pictograph.

- **Look and say. Then write.**

Developmental Writing

Learning to Know

Yolanda has yards and yards of yarn.

Objectives: Trace letter y.

Match the parts to the animal.

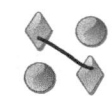

Artistic Expression and Appreciation

Learning to Be

Objectives: Identify parts of the body of farm animals.

Unit 7 — 157

- **Say what animals need and what you need.**

Physical Development and Health
Learning to Be

- **Match the objects to the lamb or to the child.**

158 Unit 7

Objectives: Find similarities between farm animals and human beings.

- **Color the beginning sound of each picture.**

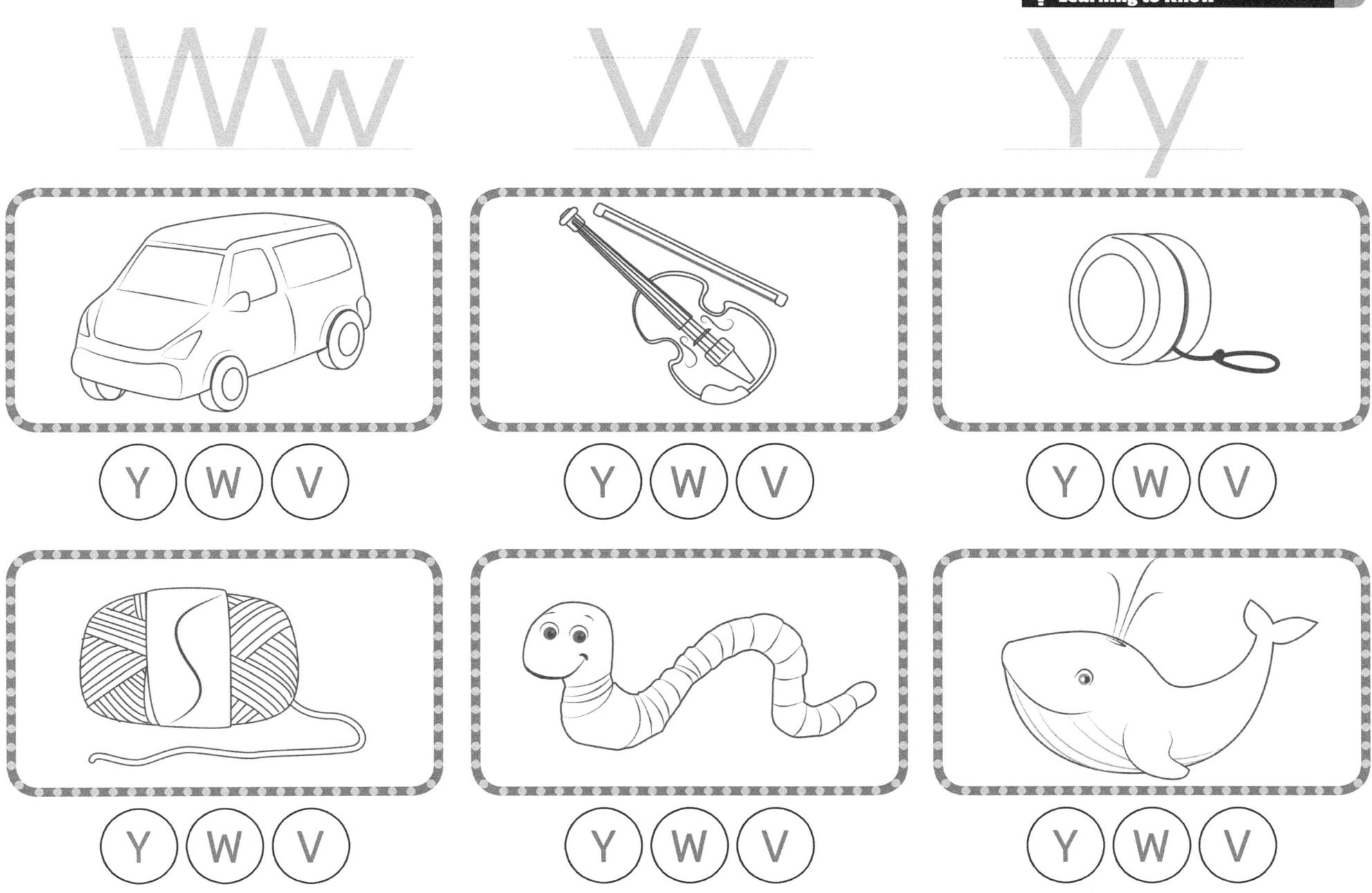

Phonemic Awareness
Learning to Know

Ww   Vv   Yy

| Y W V | Y W V | Y W V |
| Y W V | Y W V | Y W V |

Objectives: Identify initial /w/, /v/, and /y/ sounds.

- **Look at the Class Calendar. Copy the month and the year. Copy number 1.**

Mathematical Thinking
Learning to Know

| April | June | August | October | December | February |
| May | July | September | November | January | March |

Month: _____ Year: _____

Monday	Tuesday	Wednesday	Thursday	Friday	Saturday	Sunday

Objectives: Identify and write numbers to 30. Say the date.

- **Look and say. Then write.**

Developmental Writing
Learning to Know

Can the whale eat yogurt in a van?

Objectives: Trace letters w, y, and v.

Unit 7

- **Finish the drawing and fingerpaint the animals.**

  Artistic Expression and Appreciation
  Learning to Be

- **Match the animal to its products.**

162 Unit 7

Objectives: Fingerpaint farm animals and the products they give us.

- **Match the animals to where they live.**

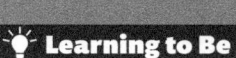

- **Draw another animal in its home.**

Physical Development and Health

Learning to Be

Objectives: Reflect on how both animals and people need a house.

Unit 7

- **Match the objects that start with *q*.**

Phonemic Awareness

Learning to Know

Qq

164 Unit 8

Objectives: Identify the initial /q/ sound.

- **Write how many. Circle more than 10. Cross out less than 10.**

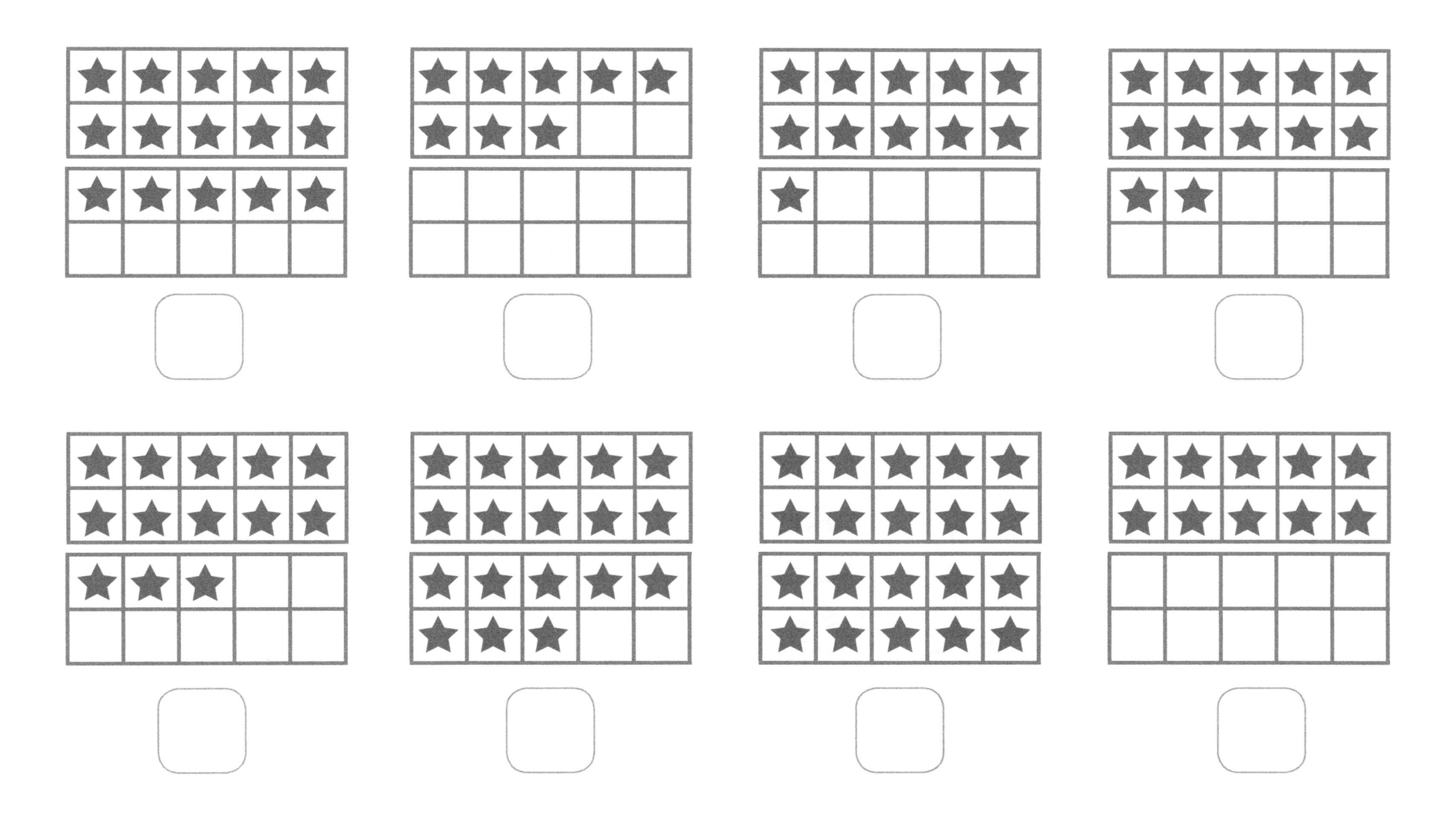

Mathematical Thinking

Learning to Know

Objectives: Identify more and less.

- **Look and say. Then write.**

Developmental Writing

Learning to Know

The queen is quiet.

Objectives: Trace letter *q*.

- **Make a collage about your town.**

Artistic Expression and Appreciation
Learning to Be

- **Show your picture to your friends.**

Objectives: Use different techniques, materials, and tools to represent their town.

Unit 8

- **Look at the picture and color the traffic lights.**

Physical Development and Health
Learning to Be

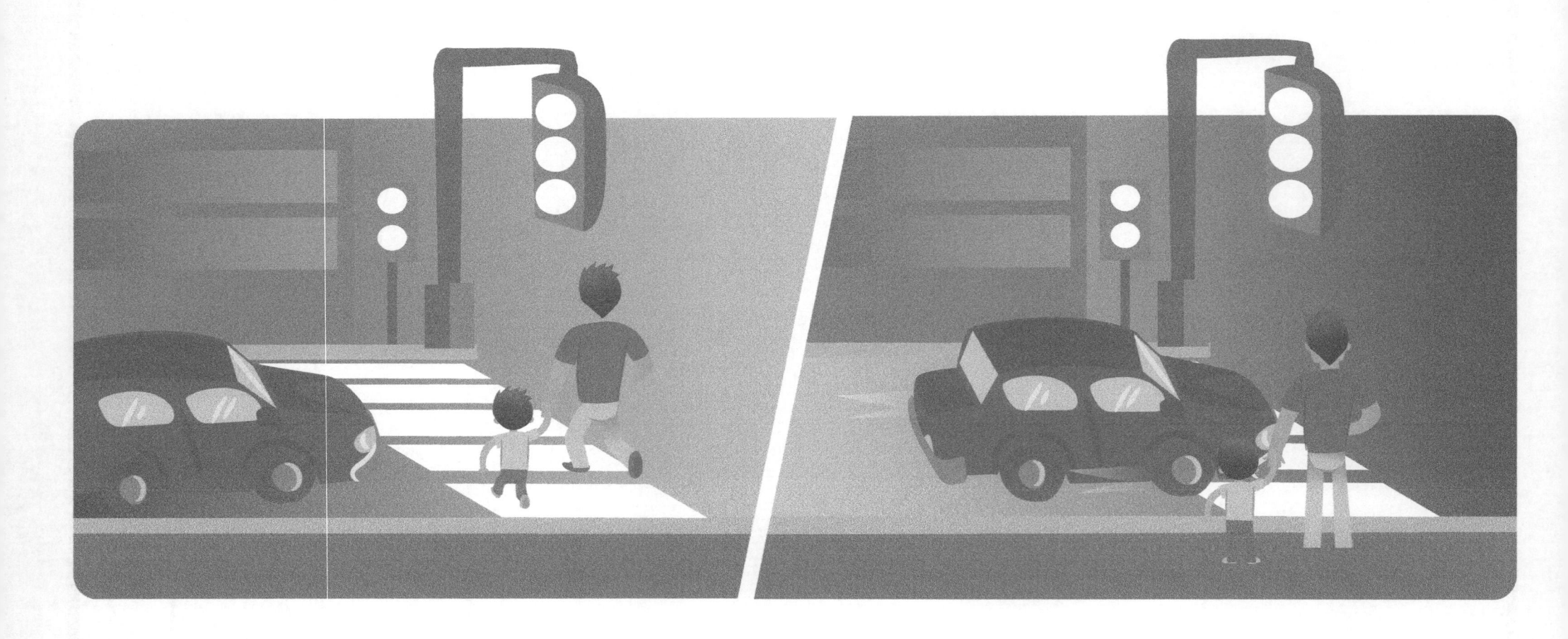

168 Unit 8

Objectives: Understand and follow rules.

- **Look at the words and color the pictures that have an X.**

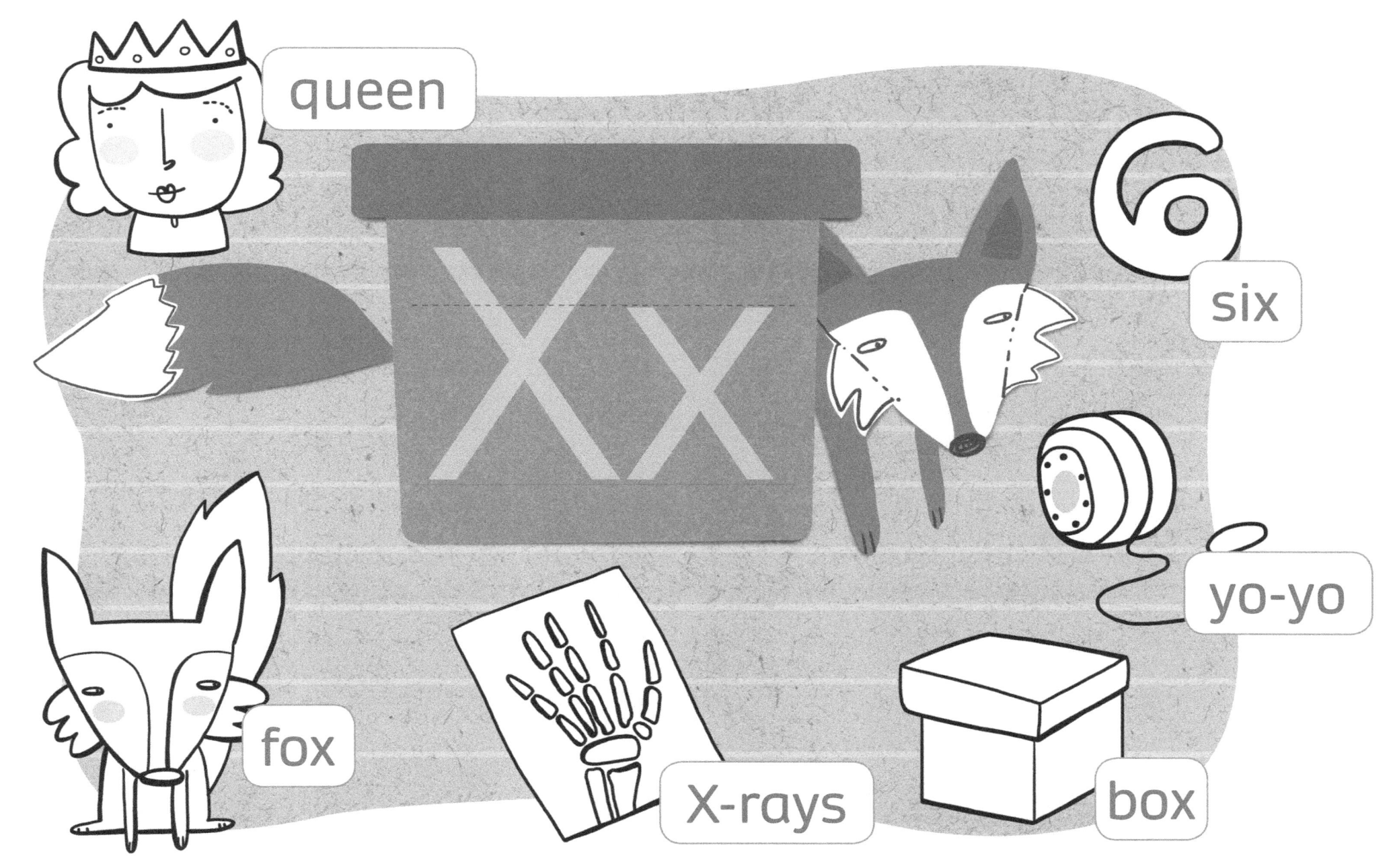

Phonemic Awareness
Learning to Know

queen

Xx

six

fox

X-rays

yo-yo

box

Objectives: Identify the /x/ sound.

Unit 8

Complete the pattern.

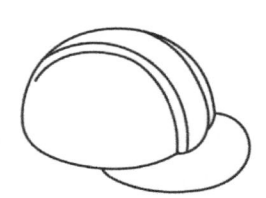

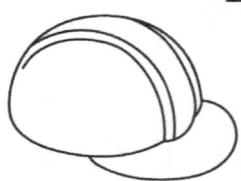

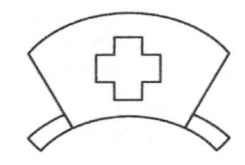

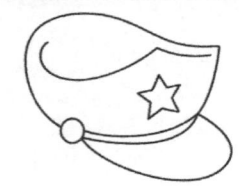

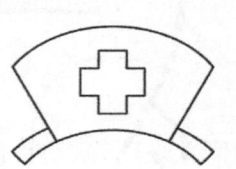

Mathematical Thinking
Learning to Know

Objectives: Extend complex patterns.

- **Look and say. Now write.**

Six foxes in six boxes.

Objectives: Trace letter x.

- **Match the objects to the workers.**

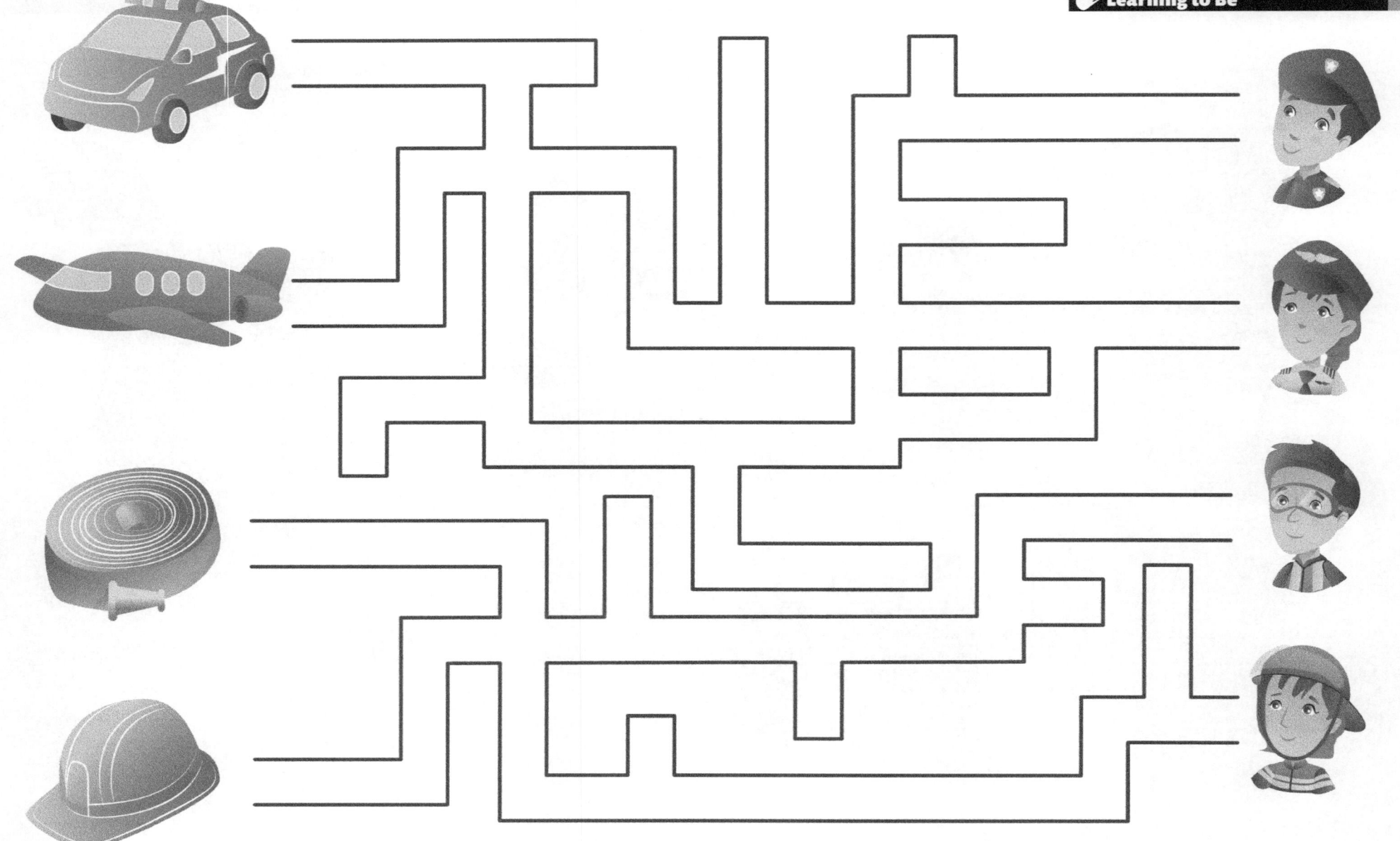

- **Choose your favorite community worker. Act out.**

172 Unit 8

Objectives: Act out a community worker.

- **Color the garbage can.**

- **Paste pictures of trash on the can.**

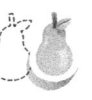

Objectives: Respect others and the environment.

Physical Development and Health
Learning to Be

Unit 8

- **Circle the pictures that start with z. Trace the letters.**

Phonemic Awareness

Learning to Know

Zz

Unit 8

Objectives: Identify the initial /z/ sound.

- **Count and color to make 10. Write.**

0 1 2 3 4 5 6 7 8 9 10 11 12 13 14 15 16 17 18 19 20

Mathematical Thinking
Learning to Know

5 + 5 = 10 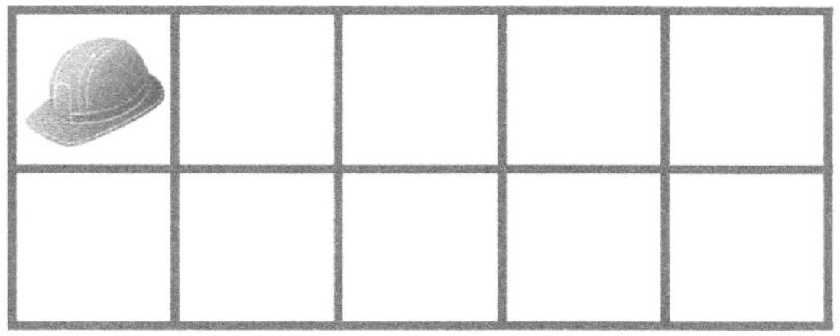   1 + 9 = 10   __ + __ = __

- **Draw.**

3 + __ = 10    __ + __ = 10    __ + __ = 10

Objectives: Make tens.

Unit 8

● **Look and say. Then write.**

Developmental Writing

Learning to Know

The zebra zigzags in the zoo.

Objectives: Trace initial z.

Make a collage of community workers.

Artistic Expression and Appreciation

Learning to Be

Objectives: Use different techniques, materials, and tools to represent community workers.

Unit 8

- **Match the signs to the shapes.**

Physical Development and Health
Learning to Be

- **Play.**

178 Unit 8

Objectives: Understand and follow rules.

- **Match the objects to the *q*, *x*, and *z*.**

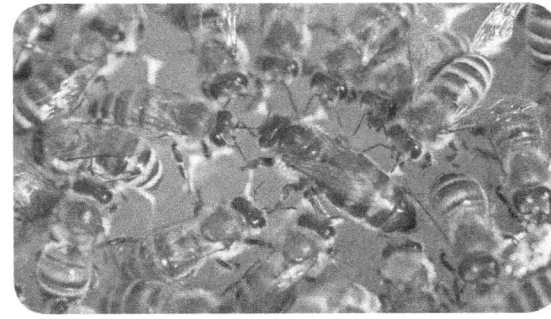

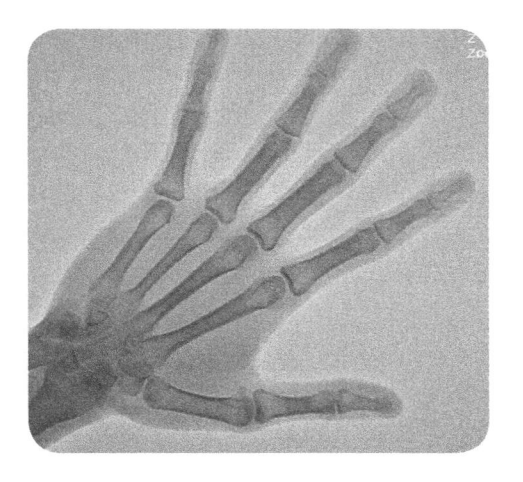

Qq

Xx

Zz

Phonemic Awareness

Learning to Know

Objectives: Identify /q/, /x/, and /z/ sounds.

Unit 8 **179**

- **Look at the Class Calendar. Copy the month and year. Write the dates.**

April	June	August	October	December	February
May	July	September	November	January	March

Month: _____ Year: _____

Monday	Tuesday	Wednesday	Thursday	Friday	Saturday	Sunday

Mathematical Thinking — Learning to Know

Objectives: Identify and write numbers to 30. Say the date.

- **Look and say. Then write.**

Developmental Writing

Learning to Know

A zebra asking questions in a box.

Objectives: Trace letters q, x, and z.

- **Draw yourself as a community worker.**

Artistic Expression and Appreciation

Learning to Be

Objectives: Use different techniques, materials, and tools to represent community workers.

- **Color what the children do to be safe.**

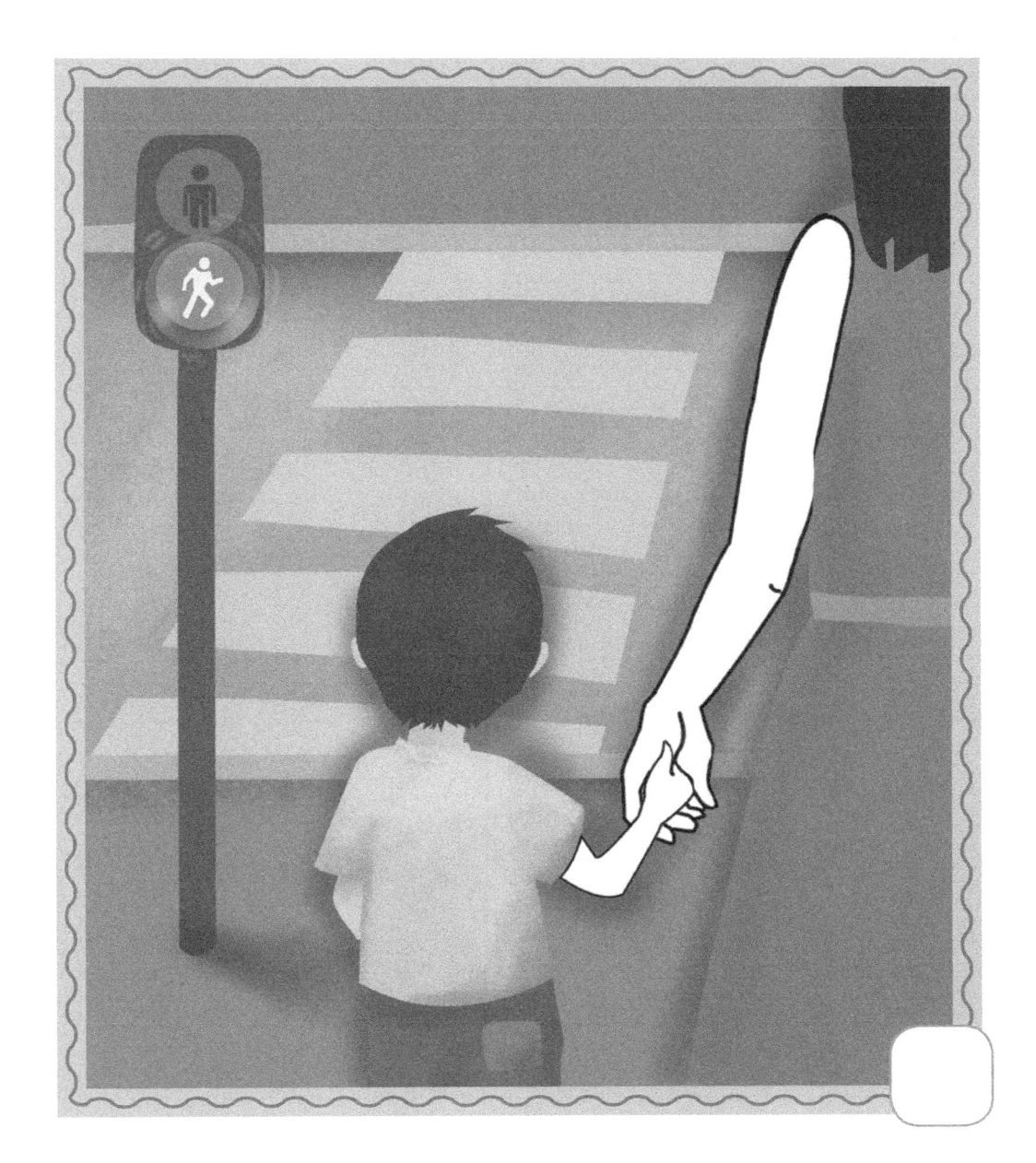

Physical Development and Health

Learning to Be

- **Check what you do to be safe.** ✔

Objectives: Understand and follow rules.

Unit 8